WHAT OTH

In her new book, The Porpoise Driven Life, my friend Melody Baran has given each of her readers a cool drink of living water. Filled with much more than its many clever and entertaining aquatic metaphors, her book is an upbeat, encouraging exhortation for anyone seeking to know God and His Son more intimately. Born out of her own journey and challenges, Melody's work paints an honest picture of the great adventure life is when one looks to God and the Lord Jesus for comfort, direction, and genuine fulfillment. Whether or not you have a porpoise, you certainly can find your godly purpose in life.

Reverend John A. Lynn

President, The Living Truth Fellowship

Struggling to know why God put you here? Don't feel alone. Melody Baran pens a practical, well-thought- out and honest guide to honing in on your life purpose, including some foundational prerequisites we would be wise to meditate on and learn. Your true journey can begin now.

David Yates

Filmmaker, TV Producer, CEO

If you're interested in finding or solidifying your purpose and are ready to embark on a new adventure starting at the intersection of God and science, this inspiring and practical book is a must-read!

Aaron Anastasi

Best-Selling Author, Transformational Coach

Entrepreneur, Voice Instructor, and Actor

'The Porpoise Driven Life' is an inspiring account on how The Lord works throughout our lives. It drives home real-life examples of how humans can be oblivious to His workings, only to realize He is with us all along! The way the author ties scripture to her experiences is inspirational and her life's journey is both edgy and exciting!

Kane Rigney
Worship Pastor and Marine Scientist

No matter where you are in your journey with the Lord, The Porpoise Driven Life offers deep encouragement and insight to assist along the way! Though it is a winsome and easy read, it is deeply profound and motivating. I recommend this book for Christians both young and old who seek to take their walk to the next level!

Janet Speakes
Editor and Christian Community Connector

This book is a treasure! Full of powerful lessons, heartfelt encouragement, and great wisdom, it's sure to help readers from countless walks of life get in touch with their purpose in God's plan for the ages.

Renee Dugan
Author, Editor and Writing Mentor

This is a hugely encouraging book that uses helpful illustrations and prayers to allow us to look into our lives and ask what we have been holding onto that we may need to let go of, and how we could move forward with God. Melody's uplifting style invites us to see the truth of the gospel and ultimately points us to God's goodness.

Michelle Brooks
Friend

It's awesome to see a college student from the cornfields of Indiana pursue her God given dreams and now through her writings help so many understand the truth of who God is through her faith journey, scripture and prayer. From the very beginning she pulls you in with creative story telling and then brings you to asking yourself very important life questions that you might not have even realized you were already asking yourself. Take a moment and let Melody take you on a journey to discovering who God is and who you are!

Ethan Parker

Director of Harborside Music, Worship leader, Speaker, Mentor

Many plans are in a man's mind, but it is the LORD's purpose for him that will stand. Proverbs 19:21 - I have known Melody for over 20 years and I have never been in her presence that she didn't make me laugh at her dry humor. Her humor comes from the joy with which she has embraced God's purpose for her life as demonstrated in the telling of her story in these pages. You will experience the roller coaster of emotions with her as she talks about the highs and lows in her life. Your life will be blessed in the reading of it to discover that God's purpose and plan for our lives is unstoppable.

Roy & Myra Price

Latin Deaf Services, Inc.

Published by Two Penny Publishing
850 E Lime Street #266, Tarpon Springs, Florida 34688

For permission requests and ordering information, email the publisher at:
info.twopenny@gmail.com

Cover Photography by: Melody Baran
Book Design by: Jodi Costa
Cover Design by: Adrian Traurig

ISBN (book): 978-1-950995-06-6
ISBN (ebook): 978-1-950995-08-0

FIRST EDITION

For more information about Melody Baran or to book her for your next event or media interview, please contact her representative at: info.twopenny@gmail.com

ACKNOWLEDGMENTS

Thanks to my earthly father Walter Baran who has been such a great example of dedication in instilling great tools for life starting with my favorite lesson: that our attitude is the thing we always have the power and freedom to choose. Dad has been there for me and helped me navigate so many of my waves in life and I will always be grateful for his steadfast love and encouragement.

I would also like to honor my dearly-missed sweet and beautiful mom Anne who always dreamt of being a Florida girl during this life. She would've been so proud of her three kids.

Endless thanks goes to my family being a God-loving, fun-having, outdoor-seeking, bad pun-telling, and encouragement-giving group. I thank my big brother Lance, the original animal-loving naturalist in the family and my first fishing buddy, who is among the few who can occasionally outdo me in a pun competition. Oceans of gratitude go to my big sister Dawn who initially brought God's truth to me and has been a close and wonderful blessing in my life for as long as I can remember. She is also the one who originally came up with the term "Oceans of Love" which I shamelessly use all the time. I am also so blessed by and grateful for my wonderful praying sis-in-law Angie, my intelligent and talented nephews Jesse and Taylor, my beautiful and powerful niece Caleigh, little Miss E., and Elie G.

Humble gratitude I have for all of the people who have prayed for me and for this book to be something that's inspiring, uplifting, and helpful. May God take this book wherever He wants it to go.

There is a vast pool of people with whom I've had the pleasure of working side by side in almost every sort of imaginable scenario in the efforts of animal care and stranding response and it is an enormous challenge to mention everyone in the reasonable space of this page. Many are the wonderful people that have been kind, gracious, and helpful to me, even in my early years of floundering around as a marine biologist. Like family to me are: the Kobernas; Chris and Melissa, some of the best friends I could ask for; and Colby and Nathan who are the best Godsons to me. Also, I am so grateful for the decades of friendship, love, support, and connection with Terri Hepburn, Amy Baird, Dennis Kellenberger, Angie (and Mum) and Mike Gabbert, Barb Farrell, Elaine and Fred Brisard,

Jennifer Blackburn, Abby and Elly Stone, Brett Stone, Rhonda Bailey, Cathy Garnier-Janota, Nadine K., Kim Beamer, Tim Hudson, Jeff Wilborn, the Derdowskis, the Redlows, the Bordeauxs, the Brandts, and so many more than could easily be named here.

For the love, encouragement, support, friendship, and seeing the best in me, I am thankful to Janet Hamady, Robin Moore, Donna Stone, Michelle Brooks, Karen Preston, Janet Speakes, Anna Sullivan, and my mer-man Wayne Owens.

To John Schoenheit and John Lynn I am forever thankful for decades of truly powerful bible teachings that have been intellectually satisfying, practical, inspiring, and have helped me to grow in spirit and in truth.

I am so grateful for all of my shipmates near and far (you know who you are), land and sea, on whale-studying voyages a-plenty. You are like family to me. You're an amazing group of people and I've been so blessed to be out on the high seas with you.

I am thankful for team members and participants at Breakthrough training for courageous and inspiring living.

For truly helpful involvement with this book I thank:

Renee Dugan for her early-on editing eye as well as the consistent and powerful encouragement that she infused into my heart and my writing process along the way;

Amy Whitt for her scientific camaraderie on land and at sea and, of course, her helpful editing skills;

Heidi Malizia for her insightful feedback along the way and her skilled and detailed efforts of social media outreach;

Carol Roden, for her continued encouragement, wisdom, and humor along the way;

Aaron Ananstasi for powerful transformational coaching through this process and many others.

As for the wonderful folks at Two Penny Publishing I am exceedingly grateful to:

Tom Goodlet for helping me to fine-tune the message and for guidance and strategy;

Jodi Costa for pulling every detail together and keeping us all on track;

Sarah Williams for her efforts of bridging the varied gaps;

Adrian Traurig for a beautiful cover design

Karen Hoke for her insightful and brilliant edits that greatly improved the flow of the message.

For

The One who walks on water

and calms the wind and waves

TABLE OF CONTENTS

PORPOISE PUN DISCLAIMER

For the purpose of this book, I playfully use the term "porpoise" very loosely. It's conveniently similar to the word "purpose," and I just can't resist a good pun. Pictured on the cover of this book is a dusky dolphin off New Zealand. He/she is not a porpoise, but does a great job of representing the idea. My fellow marine scientists who read this book may want to roll their eyes at the biologically incorrect reference, but that's okay; those who know me have been rolling their eyes at my puns for many years on many ships and on many oceans. Throughout my career I have worked with bottlenose dolphins, coastal and offshore populations of dolphins, whales, and, in some instances, porpoises, including the critically endangered Vaquita in the Sea of Cortez.

Back in the day, the term "porpoise" was commonly used when referencing dolphins. I can even remember my father using the term porpoises when referring to dolphins. In my 20s and 30s, when I worked at the aquarium, my dad would call and ask, "How's the porpoise trainer?" After the umpteenth time of explaining I worked with dolphins and that there are several biological differences between the two taxa, I just gave up the losing battle and replied, "I'm fine, Daddy, how are you?" So, for these purposes, I say "porpoise."

FOREWORD

Melody Baran has written a powerful and engaging book with many important life-lessons.

The Porpoise Driven Life could be read quickly—but it should not be. It could be read without a personal journal in which to jot notes and ideas—but it should not be. I found this book to be about me—about all of us—because it is so openly and candidly about Melody, and all humans share common experiences. The Bible rightly says, "No temptation has overtaken you except what is common to humanity" (1 Corinthians 10:13 CSB). Psychologist Carl Rogers worded it this way: "What is most personal is most universal."

Indeed, those feelings that are so incredibly personal that we often do not share them—perhaps are afraid to share them—are the same feelings everyone else has, so when we do finally share them people instantly recognize the unity we all share and instead of being driven away from us they are drawn to us. Thus, in writing about herself, Melody has written about us all.

Melody's desire to be a good and godly person has given her the energy to push through, learn from, and remember the many challenges in her life, and her experiences and her honesty in dealing with them has given her a wealth of insight about life and personal growth that can benefit others. In The Porpoise Driven Life, she draws from her lifelong love of the ocean and its creatures and her personal experiences with them, crafting these life-lessons into fresh, fun-to-read and easy-to-remember incidents and examples that remain in the mind long after the book has returned to the shelf.

One anecdote that stuck out in particular to me was how Melody's intimate experiences with buoyancy (much of her life is spent floating in a boat on the ocean, and her specialty is sea-going mammals) gave her insights of how we can be like beach balls (Really? Who knew?). We all know beach balls are difficult to keep underwater because the air in them is not as dense as the water around them. In this book, Melody points out that stress is like water, dense and high pressure, while in contrast, being peaceful keeps us light and low pressure, allowing us to pop to the surface and float above the stress. I now find myself thinking a lot about being a beach ball.

But this book is much more than a compilation of personal experiences and teachable moments; it is a challenge. Melody punctuates her stories with penetrating questions and powerful, thoughtful prayers that urge readers to rise above the weaknesses of our humanity and be greater than we otherwise would have been. For that reason, for the lessons both personal and universal, this is a book I recommend to all.

John W. Schoenheit

Spirit & Truth Fellowship International

INTRODUCTION

I've written this book for a few reasons.

Firstly, I have a desire to fulfill my God-given destiny; and I believe others who are trying to do the same could use some encouragement for the journey. I am overwhelmed with thankfulness toward my Savior and Lord Jesus Christ who made a way for the ultimate dream to come true—a rich relationship with my Creator here and now followed by an incredible eternity with Him, my Lord, and my wonderful brothers and sisters who choose to be there. I am so very thankful that He has helped me to obtain clarity to reach out and share some of the stories about God's love in my life and how He has helped me to live, and to live with purpose.

For a long while, I have felt a desire to write this book for that reason. It would be a way to honor Him in written words as well as spoken words while potentially lending encouragement and inspiration to others along the way. I can't tell you, though, how long I've been putting it off. On so many occasions, I'd enjoyed the many, many confirmations from God and encouragement from friends and family to write this book. More than a decade later, I finally got serious about it. And here it is. This is for you, my fellow searcher and striver in making a difference for God's Kingdom and richly adding to the world in ways that you and I are well-equipped to do.

Secondly, I have long had the desire to remind people about the goodness of God. Please know this is something I've believed through multiple trips from the tops of mountains to the depths of Death Valley and back again. I know God is good—not because circumstances were easy, because they weren't. In fact, it was in the most tragic and darkest times in my life that I was most powerfully able to defend God's goodness for the sake of those around me. I'll talk more about this a little later in the book. God says He is love. And love is very good. I believe Him, and I trust Him; and I know He has our best interest at heart and wants good things for you and me. He is trustworthy; and when you earnestly search for truth, He will help you find it.

To doubt the goodness of God is to get caught in the loop of doubt that Eve did when she and Adam inadvertently traded away their God-given authority in the Garden of Eden. Let's decide for ourselves we are not going to be deceived by this lie. Not anymore. That deception is a threat to our living out the fullest that God has for us. Each of us has to settle this matter in his/her own heart. What a relief it is when we don't have to wrestle with this idea but just know for a fact it is true. It's okay to ask God for answers for certain things. He's not afraid of our questions; and He tells us to ask, seek, and knock. And when we do, it will be opened to us. He tells us to ask for wisdom. Let's do that. The Glory of God is to conceal a matter and the glory of Kings to search it out (Proverbs 25:2). Let's be the Kings and Priests He has called us to be.

Thirdly, I want to encourage people to be diligent in finding their purpose in God's Purpose. It is in His Purposes that we thrive. For the longest time, I was Porpoise-driven. I spent almost all of my energy, time, and other resources working to rescue marine life (primarily dolphins and whales, but also sea turtles and other marine life). It was and is, in so many ways, one of the greatest jobs in all the world. I have some great stories few other people in the world could tell, and I promise to tell some of the good ones. As amazing as those experiences were, I knew some really important work that would last into eternity was about God and His Kingdom and the people He so dearly loves. Many of these stories that I tell are from my journey as a seagoing, marine-mammal-studying biologist seeking and finding my purpose in Him.

Many people believe God and science are at odds with one another; however, we can be assured that the God who created the universe knows better than any of us exactly how it works. Because God made it all, from subatomic particles to galaxies, spiritual realms, the unmatchable workings of the human brain, the power of language, and puppies, He is not surprised by the things we are.

If you are already operating in your purpose for the current season of your life, I hope to provide you encouragement for the journey.

If you are still looking for your purpose, I hope some of the things I write will be helpful in establishing a starting place for you to discover it.

I want to make God smile, and I imagine you do also.

So, let's embark on this purposeful voyage together. Let's explore the goodness of God and some of the many good plans He has for us in His will.

PART ONE

GETTING UNDERWAY

CHAPTER ONE

WHAT'S THE PURPOSE?

What's the point? I was about eight or nine years old when I remember sending out a big, strong request to God. I was riding my little tan-colored Huffy girl's ten-speed bike through our neighborhood. It was a nice bike; it was a nice neighborhood, and I was a nice little girl, at least most of the time. But something just didn't make sense to me. There had to be something behind everything I saw. What's the point of it all: people, trees, grass, roads? I grew desperate to know.

My beautiful, sweet mom had cancer; and as a result, she was a bit disfigured and could not live a "normal" life for almost as long as I could remember. Her compromised state had to do mostly with prescribed cancer treatments: 14 surgeries and many chemotherapy and radiation treatments. She couldn't eat normally, talk normally, or get around normally for about six years. In addition to being scared for her and for all of us, I was often sad I didn't have a "normal" family where moms and dads were happy, healthy and didn't worry about one of them dying.

I turned the corner and went down the little street where some friends lived.

My parents knew the grown-ups, and I knew the little boy who was a couple years older and the little girl who was younger than I. I saw their father mowing the lawn. Everywhere I looked there were houses, cars in driveways or in garages, trees of various sorts, people doing things like yard work or cooking dinner, and kids playing on swing sets.

Really, what's the point? My basic understanding was that people had jobs and went to work so they could earn money and pay for their houses, cars, dinners and swing sets. As kids, our job was to go to school to learn so when we grew up, we too could get jobs and pay for houses, cars, dinners, and swing sets. So, what? Was that it? Was that all of what life was about?

It seemed like a lot of fuss, but for what? I mean, what is the value of having a house and a car, so you can go to work to pay for your house and car? It just seemed a bit circular, you know, like a dog chasing its tail. The more I thought about that loop, the more hopeless everything seemed. What if my mom were healthy and things weren't so stressful at home? Would we also just be in the not-so-merry-go-round of jobs, houses, cars, and work?

I started to mentally swoon with hopelessness. Rather than just falling off my bike right there, I did the only thing I could think to do. I sent out a distress signal to the Creator of it all.

God, if you really exist and really made all of this, what is the point of it all? Why did you make the earth and grass and people, including people who would make cars? Why are we here? If you are really out there, won't you please tell me why everything is going along the way I'm seeing it? I don't want to also start spinning my wheels, if that in fact is what all these people are doing. I don't want to live a senseless, circular life of houses, cars and jobs. God, if there is a big secret, will you please tell it to me? If there's something really important going on, won't you tell me? If there is a really big idea out there, I DON'T WANT TO MISS IT! Are all of these people missing it? Please tell me! Can't I know? What's the point? What's the purpose?

Within the next couple of years, the answers to my questions started to come. The most urgent and most important answer came first: God really, really loves us, and rescues us through Jesus, who shows us God's love; and through Him we have the most amazing, powerful and unshakable connection to God. God wants very good things for us.

My big sister had become involved in a ministry—a group of people that read, researched and lived by the Bible. They taught that God is real, loves us deeply, and wants to have a great relationship with us. He desires to help us in a very powerful way and share in His goodness. This was GREAT news to me because, honestly, I sometimes found life to be very difficult. They taught the love and power of Jesus Christ. They taught that prayer was real and powerful, but also as simple as having a conversation with God. They promoted the idea that living as a group of Christians who supported one another could be very similar to the community described in the Book of Acts.

Having learned a ton about God and the Bible, my sister shared her knowledge with me. I was so thirsty for this information that I drank it up as fast as I could! This was my foundation. Although I was occasionally, when young, exposed to traditional religion, I didn't find it fulfilling. It seemed to have more ritual and reverence for people rather than God, and the rules just didn't make sense to me. What I learned straight from the Bible was thrilling and empowering, and made so much sense. It was the beginning of the answer to my intense prayer—my plea for understanding on the meaning of life.

Deep down I had felt a tension in life I couldn't sort out. Something wanted to me to live, thrive, and be powerful and "something else" wanted me to fail, wither, and be taken out of life. What the Bible said about life was starting to make sense, explaining these juxtaposed concepts in black and white.

Throughout my life, I have come to love the fact that God does answer requests. He loves when we ask Him and He loves when we honor Him by seeking Him, His will, and His heart in every matter.

I was delighted to learn that life is about SO MUCH MORE than jobs and houses and cars or even the day to day turmoil or joys in life. Not all of the answers to my questions came at once. Sometimes I found He would answer portions of my questions through people. Other times I would receive the answers from checking it out myself in His instruction book—by reading, researching, and listening to many people whose passion it is to study and teach the scriptures. Occasionally my answers came simply by letting my heart connect to Him, listening and learning His ways. In the quietness of my heart, He would show me a fresh thought, provide hope for a new outcome to a situation, or incline me to take a certain action. I learned to love His lead.

Many specific answers came from people who pointed me to books, articles and Bible studies that clearly lay out intellectually satisfying discussions about the coexistence of God and science.

I was so incredibly relieved to learn there is immense Purpose. We, as children of God, have an amazingly important identity and an irreplaceable role to play in the most incredible story ever written.

We are called into a loving relationship with the Creator of the Universe and our Lord Jesus Christ, who paid the ultimate price and leads us in our purpose.

We are called to be witnesses of the Good News bringing people to freedom through what God has done through Jesus Christ.

We are called to use our prayers, faith, and obedience to bring Heaven to earth.

We are called to use our voices and abilities to show the world who God is and to bring about His will in our lives and in this time.

We are called to stand with God and our Lord Jesus Christ, and therefore, stand against evil.

God had Plan A with the First Adam and Eve in the Garden; then the fall happened, and things were tainted with sin.

Jesus Christ, the Last Adam was Plan B, the one man who could and would bring on God's plan of redemption for all of creation. Jesus in perfect obedience served as the only sacrifice to fully pay the price of redemption. God raised Him from the dead and He is functioning as the Head of a body of followers. Until He comes back to completely fix the mess.

We are Plan BC (Body of Christ), the ones with whom Jesus Christ's power and authority are shared as his representatives in the world at this current time in History.

All this is from God, who reconciled us to himself through Christ and
gave us the ministry of reconciliation:
that God was reconciling the world to himself in Christ,
not counting people's sins against them.
And he has committed to us the message of reconciliation.
We are therefore Christ's ambassadors,
as though God were making his appeal through us.
We implore you on Christ's behalf: Be reconciled to God.
God made him who had no sin to be sin for us,
so that in him we might become the righteousness of God.
2 Corinthians 5:18–21

Where are you hungry for God's love and understanding?
What about life is the most perplexing part?
What answers have you sought from God?
What answers have you received?
How did those answers come?

Ask and it will be given to you; seek and you will and;
knock and the door will be opened to you.
For everyone who asks receives;
the one who seeks finds; and to the one who knocks,
the door will be opened.
Matthew 7:7–8

PRAYER

Father, thank You for showing us that we have an immensely important role to play in the greatest story that ever existed. Clarify our vision, Father, and let Your light cut through the obscurity of everyday life in such a way that we see the urgency, intensity, and purpose of life. The enemy would have us lulled into the complacency of a purposeless life; but we know You have a purpose planned, and You offer us Life! You made a way for us to live fully, freely, and unhindered. You offer us the help to be fully alive and gainfully employed by Your Glorious Kingdom. We will not be distracted by the mundane. Let us live in Your power to the fullest and help us to be who you created us to be. We ask these things in the name of Jesus Christ. Thank You for all these things, in the name of Your Son Jesus Christ.

CHAPTER TWO

PRE-VOYAGE QUESTION TO SETTLE:

IS GOD REALLY GOOD?

At the end of life, each of us must answer the question,

'Whose story captured my soul?'

JAMES MACDONALD

Will we believe God's story?

For God so loved the world that He gave His one and only Son,

that whoever believes in Him shall not perish but have eternal life.

John 3:16

Or

Will we believe one of Satan's stories?

That God is not really all that good; and by the way, what about all the mess in the world? **(Deadlock)**

That there is no God? **(Deception)**

That there is no major thing at stake if I just choose not to choose? **(Distraction)**

That we have to measure up to man-made standards (works) to be good enough? **(Discombobulation)**

That there are many ways to achieve salvation other than what God said? **(Distortion)**

There is no neutral ground in the universe. Every square inch, every split second is claimed by God, and counterclaimed by Satan.

C. S. LEWIS

"The thief comes only to steal and kill and destroy; I have come that they may have life, and have it to the full," says Jesus in John 10:10

God's mission: Redeem us, save us, and give us eternal life, bless us exceedingly abundantly...

Now to Him who is able to do far more abundantly than all that we ask or think, according to the power at work in us, ...

Ephesians 3:20

It's all in the Names.

What are some of God's names?

ABBA	Father
ADONAI	Lord
EL SHADDAI	God Almighty
ELOHIM	The Creator
YAHWEH -RAPHA	The Lord Who Heals
EL DEAH	God of Knowledge
EL ROI	The God Who Sees
YAHWEH-TSIDKENU	The Lord Our Righteousness
YAHWEH-JIREH	The Lord Will Provide

When God first defined his name for Moses in Exodus 34:6 he used the following terms to describe his character:

"And he passed in front of Moses, proclaiming, "The LORD, the LORD, the compassionate and gracious God, slow to anger, abounding in love and faithfulness…"

In contrast, what are the Devil's various names?

The Deceiver, the Accuser of the Brethren, Father of Lies

Satan's mission: Steal, Kill, Destroy, oh yeah, and to Deceive.

What are the raw economics at play here? Ask the question, "If I doubt the goodness of God, who benefits?"

Could it be Satan?

(I am saying that in my head in the best Saturday Night Live Church Lady voice. Some of you are saying this with me right now, just because if you've ever heard it before, it's irresistible.)

Yes, Satan is the one who benefits when we doubt God's goodness.

Satan probably loves to see that same old worn-out original lie work over and over and over again! Don't buy it! Stop letting that one stall you in the battle. Let us stick our God is Good flag in the ground and not give up that territory anymore!

For me, it was critical to get clear on this foundational issue so I could really join God in His voyage. After all, how could I grow in faith, increasingly trust Him, and rely on His protective lead if I had sneaking suspicions about His goodness?

If we are continually caught up in this battle—or confusion about whether or not this is a battle—we miss the real things to which we should be paying attention. Allowing this question to trip us up is how we let ourselves get derailed from the richness of a relationship with God and our Lord Jesus Christ; and our deeper purposes and God-given destinies are diminished, undermined or forsaken altogether.

I want more, and I know you do also.

Think about how believing Satan's lie dilutes our clarity so that we don't bother to invite God's power into our lives. If we are rolling around in doubt, how can we also have the faith that God will be working "… *in all things for the good of those who love Him and are called according to His purpose.*"? (He really says that in Roman 8:28!)

Feeling hurt, let down, done-wrong, robbed or injured may obscure our impression of God's goodness. How then can we manage to be obedient to the One who loves us the most if we doubt His goodness and question His intentions? You can see how the Devil is hoping to unravel us and render us ineffective in being the Sons and Daughters of God that we are called to be.

Certain situations challenge even seasoned believers. I'm talking about the things in the world that are clearly NOT good. Why are there starving children? Why is there so much corruption in the world? Why do evil people seem to get away with doing horrific things? Why do innocent people suffer? Why is there sickness and death? If there is a loving God, why does life sometimes look like a battlefield?

Maybe it's because sometimes it really is a battlefield! There are some clear examples of the work of someone whose mission is to steal, kill and destroy.

There are subtler topics as well. Think about these types of conversations:

Well-meaning Christians try to determine whether or not they believe someone was saved. "That criminal repented in the last 5 minutes of his life and he gets salvation?" "My loved one was such a good person and he/she is not going to be saved because I didn't hear him/her profess Jesus?" God knows peoples' hearts better than we do. He is loving and gracious (even more than we probably are). We can trust Him to judge. It is dangerous when we start judging God based on our assumptions of how we think He is going to judge. Yes, we know the Bible says many things about it all. We have to decide for ourselves who and what we will choose to obey. We also have the loving responsibility to share with others—especially our loved ones with whom we have intrinsic influence—what we know to be true.

This type of conversation, "Is God really good?" is a common place for people to start floundering around in the murky, muddy waters of doubt. Time is short. Don't allow yourself to get stuck in that mud. Remember, to doubt the goodness of God is to get caught in the loop of doubt as Eve did when she and Adam inadvertently traded away their God-given authority in the Garden of Eden.

Decide that you are not going to be deceived by this lie. Make the determination that this lie is not going to be used to bench you and keep you from playing on the winning team.

It is a temptation of the Adversary to question the goodness of God. Be aware of this temptation so you can escort it out rather than giving it a seat.

There are answers to all of these questions. Some are easy; some are much more challenging, and more thorough study is needed to continue to make sense of things. Sure, pursue excellence in your understanding of God and the claims He makes. He's not worried about His case being shaky. He'll help you understand when you ask Him.

Keep in mind, there's what people say, what God says, and what people say God says. They are sometimes three different things. You really have to pay attention to what is actually being said by whom. The scope of Scripture gives context for this being a fallen world.

We know that we are children of God,
and that the whole world is under the control of the evil one.
1 John 5:19

For our struggle is not against flesh and blood, but against the rulers,
against the authorities, against the powers of this dark world and
against the spiritual forces of evil in the heavenly realms.
Ephesians 6:12

It is no wonder so much of what we see going on in the world is NOT good.

The big deal here is that we have a very important role to play in this world for God's Kingdom. It's an awe-inspiring and sobering realization that we have an irreplaceable role in the greatest story in existence. We can make a huge impact, and God indeed wants us and needs us to do so! We are to be God's co-laborers. We are to be in partnership with Him.

For we are laborers together with God:
ye are God's husbandry, ye are God's building.
1 Corinthians 3:9 KJV

This floors me!

On one hand, that verse completely woos me, because God loves us so much that He has given us real responsibility and a sharing in some of life's outcomes. On the other hand, the verse terrifies me with its weight and responsibility. Aptly so, though, it has become my biggest inspiration to ignite some courage and step up and do some things for God and His kingdom.

As God's fellow workers we urge you not to receive God's grace in vain.
2 Corinthians 6:1

How?

Our perfect example is Jesus. He is the perfect representation of God's goodness. He healed the sick, made the lame walk, opened blind eyes, kicked out demons, loved people, taught people, fed people, and demonstrated God's goodness everywhere He went.

In the past God spoke to our ancestors through the prophets at many times and in various ways, but in these last days he has spoken to us by his Son,
whom he appointed heir of all things,
and through whom also he made the universe.
The Son is the radiance of God's glory and the exact representation of his being,
sustaining all things by his powerful word.
After he had provided purification for sins,
he sat down at the right hand of the Majesty in heaven.
So he became as much superior to the angels as the name
he has inherited is superior to theirs.
Hebrews 1:1-6

In life there have been so many voices that have told me:

Who are you that you could make a difference?

No one cares what you have to say!

Making a difference is for other people, not you!

You'll never be all of your potential, so why try?

You are not of value!

To all of these voices, and a few choice others, I now say "NO."

My value, and yours, is determined by a loving God who holds us dearer than we can imagine. He already proved His love for us by the extraordinary sacrifice He made to save us. Let's honor Him by seeing ourselves the way He sees us. Let's follow Jesus' lead.

There are some extremely powerful and intellectually satisfying resources out there that show God is good despite our experience of the world. When we truly know that He is good, it's easier to decide that we will take a risk, make a move, remain steadfast, rely on Him, not be shaken, join Him in the voyage, and hope for good things!

Good God Resources:

Don't Blame God by Mark H. Graeser, John A. Lynn and John W. Schoenheit

The God Who Risks by John Sanders

The God of the Possible by Greg Boyd

PRAYER

Father, show me that you are good. Show me such that I am convinced beyond measure of your goodness so that I may never wrestle with that particular question again. Show me who You are to me and show me who I am to You so that I understand this powerful relationship we have. Show me and grow me so that I may become the daughter or son that You've called me to be. Let me be filled with Your wisdom so that I may see the world and its happenings the way You do. Help me to recognize your voice on all these matters so that I may understand things Your way. Illuminate the lies for me so that I can see them for what they are. Protect me from deception that tries to veil and derail. In the name of Jesus Christ, I thank You for all these things.

CHAPTER THREE

WHAT'S THE VOYAGE ALL ABOUT?

When we know who we are, it is easier to see and understand our purpose. Let's first consider who God says we are. Then, we'll consider our purpose.

OUR IDENTITY

What does God say about who each Christian is in Christ? He says we are:

Fearfully and Wonderfully Made

I praise you because I am fearfully and wonderfully made;
your works are wonderful, I know that full well.
Psalm 139:14

A Greatly Loved and Lavished Child of God

How great is the love the Father has lavished on us,

that we shall be called the Children of God!

And that is what we are.

1 John 3:1

Never Abandoned by Him

The LORD Himself goes before you and will be with you.

He will never leave you or forsake you.

Do not be afraid; do not be discouraged.

Deuteronomy 31:8

Forgiven and Completely Washed Clean

"Come now, let us reason together," says the LORD.

"Though your sins are like scarlet, they shall be as white as snow;

though they are red as crimson, they shall be like woo."

Isaiah 1:18

New

Therefore if anyone is in Christ, he is a new creation;

the old has gone, the new has come!

2 Corinthians 5:17

Rescued and Adopted Sons and Daughters

For you did not receive a spirit that makes you a slave again to fear,

but you received the Spirit of Sonship.

And by him we cry, "Abba, Father."

The Spirit himself testifies with our spirit that we are God's children.

Romans 8:15

Promised to be Resurrected

It is written: 'I believed; therefore I have spoken.

'With that same spirit of faith we also believe and therefore speak,

because we know that the one who raised the Lord Jesus

from the dead will also raise us with Jesus and present

us with you in his presence.

2 Corinthians 4:13

OUR PURPOSE

As for our purpose or our role to play, He says we are:

Masterfully Created Agents for His Goodness

For we are God's workmanship, created in Christ Jesus to do good works,

which God prepared in advance for us to do.

Ephesians 2:10

Ambassadors of Christ

We are therefore Christ's ambassadors, as though

God is making his appeal through us.

2 Corinthians 5:20

God's Co-laborers

As God's fellow workers we urge you not to receive God's grace in vain.

2 Corinthians 6:1

WHERE DO WE START?

God tells us there's a baseline way of being. I believe this is the starting place for stepping into our role. When we want to discover our purpose, we have to start where we already know He wants us. While we are anticipating what He might have as our purpose-filled step, it helps for us to be doing what He already told us we should be doing.

Look at 1 Thessalonians 5:16-18 (NIV)…

Rejoice always, pray continually,
give thanks in all circumstances;
for this is God's will for you in Christ Jesus

Let's dissect that verse for a minute…

Rejoice always: To me this means Acknowledge God and celebrate the fact that you and He know each other—this is always something to be excited about. Recognize that He loves you intensely, immensely and without limits. He is your Dad in the best possible sense of the word…and you are His precious and dearly loved, valued, and lavished kid.

Pray continually: (in all things outward and inward) We thank God for finding us, for offering to bring about His will in our lives, for forgiving us and covering us for all the ways we fall short and miss the mark, for pouring His goodness out on us because He loves us, for opening the doors that He wants open to us (and our loved ones), and for closing doors to things that would bring us harm.

Give thanks in all circumstances: No matter what is happening, we will strive to be Thankful. In so doing, even in the worst of circumstances, we will remember that He is God; He is good, and, in the end, He will bring justice, vindication, peace, comfort, retribution, and ultimate wisdom and answers. He will even raise us from the dead and lavish us with His love for eternity, inclusive of every good thing we can imagine… and then some. No matter what happens in life, God is going to make up for it! Until then, it is thankfulness that will keep us anchored so we can weather the storms of life as graciously as possible making room for others to also see His goodness, especially during our storms. Thankfulness, I believe, keeps the doors to heaven wide open and unobstructed. I like to imagine it's through tubes of thankfulness that He pours His goodness and blessings on us.

I've always viewed thankfulness as my job. When I was a kid, my dad frequently talked to me about attitude and how that was the only thing we could really control. We can't always control circumstances, but we can always control how we react to them. As I've read the Bible, I've noticed when God talks about attitude, He says a lot about thankfulness. That is the target attitude.

Practicing thankfulness and rejoicing when things are good is very helpful in keeping the thankfulness muscles toned for when things are not good.

Please note that it does not say "…give thanks FOR (emphasis mine) all circumstances;" it says "…give thanks IN (emphasis mine) all circumstances."

This is a very important distinction. It's a great thing that we are not asked to be thankful for situations, but thankful in them. The big things to be thankful for—like God being the Almighty Creator who loves us like crazy and is in the process of bringing about the ultimate victory with us on His team— should always be the context of our attitude.

I've lost sight of that idea many times. I'm not proud of my meltdowns and temper tantrums. There are times when I've leapt right off the platform of thankfulness and done a figurative cannonball into the pool of selfishness and swam around in my selfish-mess. But it's when I've managed to maintain an undertone of thankfulness throughout the storms that I can have a hopeful outlook. God is still good, and He is still God no matter how our current circumstances look.

Using Our Talents

...be transformed by the renewing of your mind. Then you will be able to test and approve what God's will is – his good, pleasing, and perfect will.

Romans 12:2

Seeking what God has been already asking of us enables us to recognize what His will is for us. Let's strive to be people that are after what God wants for us and are willing to give His way a try. Let's rejoice, pray, and be thankful. Let's put ourselves in a position to follow His lead into our purpose.

PRAYER

Father, thank You that You and You alone are worthy of our praise and adoration. Thank You that we can rejoice in our relationship with You! Thank You for all that You are to us and all that we are to You! Thank You that we can learn to pray effectively and experience the richness of relationship with You. Thank You that in all circumstances we can be thankful. Thank You for unlocking the blessings that You have for us and allowing our attitude to be continually thankful. Help us to be wise, and please give us the perspective to do this. Thank You for helping us to renew our minds and for transforming us into people that do Your will and accomplish the good that You've set before us to do… in the name of Your Son, Jesus Christ.

CHAPTER FOUR

BASIC NAVIGATION:

FROM THERE TO HERE

The pessimist complains about the wind;
the optimist expects it to change;
the realist adjusts the sails.
WILLIAM ARTHUR WARD

One of the most precious honors that I've enjoyed over the years is encouraging students, interns, young people, and a few not-so-young people in their career paths. I've mentored hundreds of interns who were working toward getting into and making a difference in the field of marine science. I had an easy time encouraging them because I was personally excited about breaking into this field. I was the underdog, after all, and it was a direct lesson from my own experience that I could pass on.

In the cornfields of Indiana, I remember my early days as a college freshman, sitting in my academic advisor's office trying to answer the inevitable advisor question: "What is it that you want to do?"

My answer, "I'd really like to be a marine biologist who studies dolphins and whales!" was not the anticipated one; and it showed on my advisor's face.

She responded, "You do realize that you are at Indiana University, right, without any coastline around. Furthermore, even if we did have a marine science program, which we don't, only a tiny percentage of people with those types of degrees even get jobs in their field."

I offered the only explanation for the apparent absurdity that I could: "Well, my dad wouldn't help pay for any out-of-state schools, so here I am. I guess I have to start here. Also, by the way, how can I be in that tiny little percentage of people that DO get those jobs? Why not me?"

There is something to be said for asking the question to the right people. Granted, sometimes you have to ask a lot of people and get a lot of "nos" or "I don't knows" before you get an occasional "yes." Sometimes you have to ask the same question to different people to find someone who thinks there might be a "yes" out there for you. They may even be able to point you in the direction of "yes" even if they themselves can't give you the "yes." Don't be surprised that the "nos" are there. Don't be afraid of the "nos," and don't be offended or put off by the "nos." Sometimes you just have to get some "nos" out of the way before you find the right "yes." We look for our "yes" floating in a sea of "nos."

My college advisor did come through for me in some important ways. She helped me find university clubs and activities and local experiences that would nicely supplement a standard biology degree. These extras helped get more tools in my tool bag and helped me to gain access to people who had similar interests during my college years. By obtaining some experiences with animals and people, animal care, and conservation, I was at least being equipped to give marine biology a try when I could manage to get myself to an ocean. I was learning to talk the talk and walk the walk in preparation for swimming the big swim.

**I am thankful for all of those who said NO to me.
It's because of them I'm doing it myself.**
ALBERT EINSTEIN

There is always something we can do right where we are to better equip us to get where we want to be. If you want to be somewhere other than where you are, then begin to put some things in place in your life which will help you to get closer to your goal. Don't avoid doing something you are passionate about simply because it seems so far away. Take a look at what you can do to prepare, improve or acquire some experience or know-how that will move you closer. If you need more information, who can you ask? If you need money or skill, what things can you do, or what amount of money can you put away for that purpose? My dad always told me, "The future belongs to those who plan for it." Let's begin to plan for the future we really want. Let's envision and move closer to what we want. Let's make sure we put a little of the tomorrow we want into our today.

To so many of those student interns, I consider myself privileged to ask them two very important questions. These, dear reader, I also ask you:

What is your dream?

We all have many dreams, goals, and desires. What is the impact you want to make on the world and your loved ones? What is important to you? Who is important to you? What is your destiny? What is your purpose? What kind of future do you want to build for yourself?

Why not you?

What stops you?

What things are you allowing to stop you? If so, why?

Taking an honest look at what is stopping us is often a very resourceful way of gaining insight into what it is we really, really want. What is it that, by laying it aside, would allow us to move into our desired future?

Competing loves are detected in the gap between saying and doing.
JAMES MACDONALD

How often do we think we know what we want but stall in the space between the saying and the doing?

If we don't know what to do next, is there a way we can learn more?

If we have not chosen to move forward into something we feel called to do, what are the competing loves?

Has fear hijacked our potential? What's the remedy? Well, taking action often diffuses fear. Really. If that doesn't sound convincing, you can just try it out.

Is there some small step we can take in the direction we want to go that will help us create momentum? When we take some steps, no matter how small, the fear we previously felt is seen from a more powerful place. Sure, new fears may appear as we continue along our paths; but when we have a system by which to move forward even in the midst of some of our fears, we can change our situation and how we view our possibilities. Keep moving. Simplify, but keep moving forward on your big, most important priorities. Pick something you have been meaning to do. Spend even as little as a few minutes per day on it. Make it a point to address this Thing, think about this Thing, ask people about this Thing, research this Thing. Just a few minutes a day is all that it takes.

After a while, the Thing becomes a series of very small things that you can do or address bit by bit rather than that one big, monstrous Thing that is just too big, too far, too unapproachable, and too involved.

I started writing this book in late 2017. I had the idea and desire to do it about 12 years before that. I'd had the inkling to maybe do something like write a book for even longer. What changed? I'd made a decision to write it; but instead of saying, "Someday, I'm going to write a book," I said, "I am going to spend a little time every day working toward my goal of finishing a draft." I initially made a commitment to spend 10-15 minutes a day on it to actively try it out. Over time, I had to modify that process a bit and try different methods that would result in my getting words onto a page.

What are the competing loves? Do we enjoy the comfort of inaction? Does inaction make it easier to avoid potential criticism? Does it feel safer to not make a move? Sure, many times it really does. Choosing not to choose, though, is still choosing. At the end of the day, we are still responsible for our choices. Sometimes our choices are connected to the choices of others; but still, we make our own choices. We choose what to stand with and what to stand against. Let's choose wisely.

We have to decide what we want most and what we are willing to be to get it. I say "be" instead of "do" because "being" connects us to our vision and our identity.

Are we willing to be the person who takes on our obstacles, fears and temptations for inaction? Are we willing to be a person who makes a commitment and sees it through to completion? Are we going to be resilient strivers to reach a future that we want? Are we going to be committed to being free and unencumbered?

Are we willing to be the Sons and Daughters God has created us to be, accepting the invitation to partner with Him, reflecting His goodness and fulfilling our part in His plan?

I regularly ask myself, "Despite my fears, distractions, and comforts, am I willing to be the person God called me to be?"

PRAYER

Father, thank You for helping me to see the hope in faith and not the fear in doubt. Help me to keep my focus on You and bring me to where You want me. Help me to lay hold of your promise that I will find You when I seek You, and that Your goodness and love will follow me all the days of my life. I know the deepest desires of my heart were placed there by You and You alone can make things possible and bring things about in magnificent ways. Help me to be obedient in the waiting, and help me to clearly see when there is something I can do to move toward my destiny. Help me to be wise and discerning, and help me to be growing in You all the way. Thank You for bringing about Your will in my life and helping me to fulfill the purpose to which you've called me. For all these things and so much more, Father, I thank You in the name of Your Son Jesus Christ.

CHAPTER FIVE

ADVANCED NAVIGATION:

FROM HERE TO THERE

Delight yourself in the LORD and He will give you the desires of your heart.

Psalm 37:4

I was about to discover that some of our heart's desires originated with God. There is a big picture we are all part of, and sometimes we have deep desires we can't always explain. He knows what inspires us and what ignites our passions and creativity. He knows what we want and how badly we want it. He knows the best way to blend our talents, interests, desires, and efforts right into His purposes. When we put God first, it enables Him to guide us through doors He's been working to open for us.

When I was 22, I moved to Florida with two suitcases. Sleeping on the couch at my big sister's place, I was able to start doing a second volunteer internship at the little aquarium down the street. For some reason, I just knew I really wanted to work there. I had done my internship there the previous summer before my senior year at college and had fallen in love with the place. I loved all of it: the people, the animals, the mission of rescue and rehabilitation, the idea of releasing animals that could live on their own, and caring for those who could not. I was ready to marry this place.

I couldn't even tell you what was so logical about it, but somehow it all happened. I planned to be a volunteer intern at the aquarium until they paid me or until I was able to get a job somewhere else that did pay something. Nonetheless, I would give it a few weeks, months, or more depending on how I could manage financially. This plan was so unlikely! When I look back on it now, I can see that my expectations were so incredibly unreasonable. A little corn girl from Indiana whose high school years concentrated on music classes (there were no oceans in Indiana, and I had to do something with my time and energy) moves to Florida with a few items of clothing, stays with sister, gets an apartment, gets a car, and tries to get a job where everyone wants to work. I joined the large group of volunteers, college interns, and local folks who, as I did, hoped to get a job there one day and who, unlike me, already had experience working there. Not only were there already many people lining up to interview for any potential openings, but the aquarium had only 12 employees at the time; and none of them were elderly or looking to retire anytime soon. The likelihood of a position becoming available was beyond reason. Thank God that hope blinds us to all the obstacles!

PURPOSES AND PORPOISES

A month or so into this game, after my shift at the aquarium, I was sitting down by the water having a talk with God, as I sometimes did. I was already thankful for all the amazing things that He worked out to this point, but a part of me was fearful that everything would come crashing down. I feared, after all this risk and effort, I'd never get a job there or anywhere else for that matter (none of the other places I'd checked were hiring either); and I'd end up looking like a fool and regret having hoped. When I was going through all the mental gymnastics, as I tend to do, I boiled everything down to "Why, God, would you let me roll around in torment wanting something so badly that I couldn't ever get?"

"God, I have no idea why I so badly want to work at this place! I can hardly stand it! How can I even dare to think they should hire me despite all the other wonderful, more qualified, better educated, and already established volunteers, interns, and graduates with more experience and college degrees from actual local universities around actual oceans with marine science programs? But You know what, God? More than this thing that I want so badly, I want what You want for me. I surrender. I can't fight Your will. I would be miserable if I tried. I'm already borderline miserable knowing I want something so badly and am terrified that, if it is not Your will, I may never get it. So, I'm going to make the decision today that I want You to take me where You want me to go. If this is not Your will for me, please show me what is, because that is what I really want to do. I'm asking for Your way above my way, even if it means giving up the aquarium." Gulp!

I felt such a light-hearted, weird relief praying that prayer. I finally put it out there for God to deal with.

The next morning as I trotted into the aquarium for my four-hour shift, I was called into "the office." My supervisor and the director wanted to see if I'd be interested in a part-time job that might become full time down the road.

"YES! Oh, my God, thank you!" I squeaked out, having a hard time controlling my excitement. I could hardly speak because I was overwhelmed. They were both smiling at me like they knew the important sense of relief this good news brought me. Later that day, near the end of my shift, I stopped into the office again. "Glad you're here," my supervisor said, "we wanted to ask if we can go ahead and make you a full-time employee?"

"Yes, of course!" I said with the biggest smile on my face. That came faster than I thought it would!

I couldn't help asking, "I'm so glad you chose me to offer this position to, but I'd really like to know why you selected me above anyone else. After all, there are so many people from which to choose, so many volunteers and interns, that have so much more experience, know-how, education, abilities, etc. Why me?"

"The answer was simple," they explained. "So many others wanted the glamorous parts of the job, but you were willing to do it all. We see that you are interested and enthusiastic about all the workings of things here, and we know we can depend on you to do a good job no matter the level of the task. Also, you are a people-person and can follow and lead. You make our jobs easier. And finally, you just seem to be the right person at the right time."

They saw the best of what I was hoping would be true about myself. As I stood there with my mouth hanging open, they added a little more explanation for me. Unbeknownst to everyone, one biologist wanted to move away to another state; and the timing of my coming on the scene and being helpful and eager seemed to match perfectly.

I was so thankful. I frequently look back on that glorious day. Not only did it carry me through some really challenging times that were to come, it gave me a gift to share with all of the interns and volunteers I mentored over the decades. It's been a pleasure to brag about God's creative way of bringing about this dream for me when people ask about my unlikely career success; it's one of my many ways of delighting in Him. If He managed to bring about this dream for me, He can certainly bring about your hopes and dreams for you.

A LIFE WITH PORPOISE

Consider some of the wonderful things in your heart. Perhaps you have some dreams, goals, desires, or visions for yourself and loved ones. Consider that God may have put them there and is willing to work with you to bring those things about. Consider that God wants to help you to prepare, grow, and lean on Him for your present and future mission. Let us set aside our fears, anxiety, doubt, and worries. As Proverbs 3:26 says, "*...for the LORD will be at your side and will keep your foot from being snared.*" Now that's worth delighting in! Imagine the possibilities and wonderful things that God may have in store for you. Trust in His abilities to get you there. And be patient.

PRAYER

Father, thank You that You've placed hopes, desires, and dreams inside of us. Thank You that You bring us from where we were to where You want us to be according to Your perfect will. Help us to see the vision of what You want for us and help us be patient and focused on the vision in the times of waiting. Thank You for the simplicity that You ask of us: That we delight ourselves in You. Thank You that You already want to give us the desires of our hearts. Thank You for the seasons of life where we can grow into the people that You want us to be. Thank You for filling us with wisdom about how to go about getting to where You want us. If we are fixated on something You don't want for us, Father, You know best; help us to redirect our attention to things that are best. Thank You for helping us grow into people that will be able to deal wisely with the positions, people, and places in our lives and destinies. Above all, Father, thank You for taking us where you want us to go, according to Your will, in the name of Jesus Christ.

CHAPTER SIX

RADIO CHECK:

LOUD AND CLEAR

In preparing for any voyage it's important to test your means and ability to communicate. We need to make sure we can both send and receive messages. God sends us lots of messages and communicates his love to us in many different ways.

While studying for my Sea School test in an attempt to get my Captain's license, I was finding fun and creative ways to procrastinate. I'm especially skilled at procrastination, distraction, and even desperate reorganization tactics when really necessary. As I was studying my little cheat sheet of nautical flags depicting the phonetic alphabet, I was quizzing myself, and looking at the meaning of each flag.

All of a sudden, I felt an urge to check out the meaning of the word LOVE in the phonetic alphabet. The phonetic alphabet is a way of speaking among sailors, navigators, pilots, air traffic controllers, military personnel, etc., where each letter of the alphabet has a certain word associated with it, so that the whole word is stated in place of the letter. This is important so that radio transmissions are not misunderstood. Anyone trained in basic radio communications is required to know the whole alphabet. You have probably heard of this in one form or another. A=Alpha, B=Bravo, C=Charlie...all the way through Y=Yankee, and Z=Zulu. There seems to be an intrinsic need for this clarity that becomes obvious when someone on the phone is trying to spell something out, and one person will say, "A as in Apple, T as in Tom, or B as in Boy..." and so on. These phonetics ensure clarity between communicators.

Also, each of these letters has an associated flag with a specific pattern, color, and design. When flown from a ship, each of these flags communicates a meaning to others in the area. For example, the flag for P=Papa is a small white square inside of a larger blue square, and it means "about to sail." W=Whiskey is a red square inside a white square inside an outer blue square and means "I need medical assistance." B=Bravo is a red flag lined with a small obtuse triangle on the right side and means "explosives." Often times to test their ability to communicate over the VHF radio, one communicator will request, "Radio check?" and the other will reply "Lima Charlie." This indicates they've heard it "Loud and Clear."

LIMA-OSCAR-VICTOR-ECHO

In looking up the flag meanings for L-O-V-E, I started with L=Lima which means "Stop instantly." Okay, a bit odd, I know...should I really stop? What then would be the point? I began to think I was wasting my time. Then the urge came again…keep going, follow it through! Okay, O=Oscar means, "Man Overboard." Very odd, indeed. Logically speaking, stopping is exactly what you do when someone is reported to have gone overboard. Actually you are supposed to decrease speed and turn to circle back to the spot where they fell overboard in order to pick them up. But stopping is the overall idea. Next is V=Victor, "I require assistance." Interesting. The plot was getting pretty thick here, although I still didn't know where this was going. STOP. MAN OVERBOARD. I REQUIRE ASSISTANCE.

Then, as I read the meaning for the last letter in the word LOVE, E=Echo, I had to really stop. I read and reread the meaning a few times because I was simply astounded.

Stop Instantly, Man Overboard, Need Assistance, and then, after reading Echo's meaning, I saw that the short story was a complete thought. E=Echo's meaning is the wrap up, grand slam, macro-detonation of the phrase's meaning:

Echo = "Altering course to starboard"

I will never forget this amazing nanosecond where the profound clarity of this enormous message hit me. For those unfamiliar with ship terms, port is left and starboard is right. Echo means "correcting course to the right." Making things right…

That whole message had me crying, laughing, and marveling. It was here in Lima, Oscar, Victor, and Echo, the whole meaning of LOVE was revealed. Walking through the message again, we get:

Lima – Stop Instantly

Oscar – Man Overboard

Victor – I Require Assistance

Echo – Altering Course to Starboard (correcting course to the right… to paraphrase, making things right and or looping back around to get us after we have fallen overboard).

Stop! Man's in trouble. He needs assistance. And things will be made right. Wow!

LOVE flags us down.

Here it is, love, in its deepest meaning, not only for rifts in human relationships but for the very salvation of mankind. Stop, man's overboard, needs assistance, and things will be made right. And in the end…. God is going to make all things right! To retrieve a man overboard, you circle back to pick him up. God has circled back to pick us up after mankind has fallen overboard. If you happen to be the "man" overboard and look up from your floating, terrified position in the cold water and you see that ship turn hard to come back and rescue you, that's got to be the biggest relief in the world. God's love is really written just about everywhere. "Ask, seek, knock," the Bible says.

Honestly, I hardly believed the "coincidence" that this message, of all the random possible messages from those phonetic alphabet flags, could line up the way it did. But, with everything else I know and continue to learn about how amazing God is…what else could I expect? Here is the message of love again, loud and clear. Not only do the heavens declare the glory of God and the skies proclaim the work of His hands (Psalm 19:1), but God's great love is also written in so many other places. I am amazed again and again. God's love for us is Loud and Clear.

No doubt there are opportunities to see God's love from so many different vantage points.

Where in life do you see God's love?

PRAYER

Father, thank You for Your glorious message of salvation and redemption and for putting reminders of it in all kinds of places. Thank You for the richness of Your love for us, and thank You for revealing Your plan for us in so many different and wonderful ways! In the event we are ever tempted to think You are uninvolved, we have a lot of evidence to prove that You are creatively and powerfully in every detail of life. The closer we look, the more we see of You! Thank You for continuing to open our eyes to Your wonders, and help us to discover and rediscover evidence of Your love and favor everywhere we go. We love you and thank You for all these things in the name of Your Son Jesus Christ.

PART TWO

THE VOYAGE

CHAPTER SEVEN

BEING A GOOD SHIPMATE

One of the hardest jobs we'll ever have is relating to people. As a biologist at a public aquarium, I used to do a lot of presentations, answer questions, mentor people, and do interviews about the marine animal rescue work that we did. People would always ask:

What is the hardest part of your job?

Is it the long, unpredictable hours? Is it being on call 24/7? Is it braving the elements or doing animal rescues in adverse weather conditions? Is it being up all night in the water with sick sea animals? Is it the low pay? Is it the physical struggle to remain in the water when you are tired and hungry… at 2 am during a thunderstorm… and your arms are cramping from hours of supporting a dolphin which can't swim on its own? Is it the fight to get this important work funded and well represented?

No.

While we were never short of challenges or tough situations, those were not the hardest to deal with, by a long shot. Difficulties abound, but the answer is not even in that ball park. The answer to that question, when finally given, was at first shocking to many people, then most always led to the universal head nod of acceptance.

The most challenging part of the job was…dealing with people. Nearly everyone can relate to this. Competition was intense, especially in this field; and it was easy to become a workaholic, because you had the sense that everyone was ready to replace you if you made a mistake or failed to meet a challenge. Another obstacle among my co-workers was a lot of power struggles about who was in charge of what. Not-for-profit work was a labor of love. People were not in it for the money; I believe some were in it for something else: a sense of power, glamour, attention, or popularity. Motives, including my own, were always in question, and often it felt like people were after a sense of superiority. Lines of responsibility were not clearly drawn, and it left us clamoring for our areas of charge and continually stepping on each other's toes. One battle with a particular coworker lasted for many years, and I always felt he was looking to get me fired even during the times when he was not openly saying as much. It seemed there was plenty of peer-to-peer scrutiny. I frequently wondered how easy it would be to improve the world if not for all the infighting, political games, and dysfunctional nonsense that permeated the workplace.

Leading a volunteer team was also challenging. Many volunteers were awesome to work with, and I still maintain friendships with many of them. There were others who were never happy and were continually critical of my leadership. Getting along with people is usually where the rubber meets the road.

What is to be done?

Love your neighbor as yourself.

Mark 12:31

Do to others as you would have them do to you.

Luke 6:31

Notice, He did not say "like others as you like yourself." He said "love." Love means you can treat a person with kindness and respect whether or not you like him/her. We can treat individuals as we would want to be treated without actually liking them! That should be very liberating! Brilliant, really!

We naturally love others better when we know how to love ourselves well. There are plenty of ways to do this.

BE A PERSON OF INTEGRITY

Honor your word. Keep your word. When you can't keep it, acknowledge it; and take action to make a new plan and new commitment. People respect people who take themselves and others seriously when it comes to making and keeping promises (or your word). Do what you say you are going to do. Follow through. Be someone who can trust yourself, and others will also trust you.

In a training I attended called *Breakthrough*, I learned some very important things about transformation. One of the most important lessons I learned was about honoring your word. Although I had a vague and general respect for the concept, it was during this training that I became keenly aware of it. Relationships thrive or wither on kept or broken promises. What really got my attention was this Bible verse which illuminates this relational principle:

Hope deferred makes the heart sick, but a longing fulfilled is a tree of life.
Proverbs 13:12

Hope deferred is an unfulfilled promise which leads to a sick heart and the degradation of a relationship. A longing fulfilled, a promise kept, is life-giving to a relationship. Therefore, fulfilled or broken promises are either life or death to a relationship.

BE GENUINE

Another way to be better at relating to people is to be honest. Bring your real self to relationships. No one likes a phony. Most people have pretty good BS-detecting abilities. When someone's story doesn't line up with his/her life or actions, people are unwilling to get close or let their own guard down because they cannot trust what they see or hear. How are we supposed to experience the richness of how God intended relationships to be when we are continually scrambling to present an image or straining to read through a smokescreen? Let's not stand in our own way. Also, just as importantly, don't stand in the way when others are trying to love us.

To be known and loved is our deepest desire. "Jesus knows me, this I love," reads a wall hanging at my friend's house. It's a clever flip of the more widely known "Jesus loves me, this I know...", but just as telling of the truth.

Sometimes it's easy, and natural, to get caught up in trying to uphold an image when relating to others. Most of us want to be well thought of; it can be difficult to let go of what others think about us, especially if you're like I am, with a people-pleasing background.

Larry Winget, an author known as the "Pitbull of Personal Development", in his book titled *Grow a Pair* wrote, "Honesty is not the best policy; it's the ONLY policy. If you want to be known as a person who has a pair, show up, tell the truth and let go of the outcome."

HAVE HEALTHY BOUNDARIES

I had a habit of over-committing and under-performing; it was like an autopilot setting that I could not turn off. However, when I dug in and did some personal growth work, I discovered this way of doing things was really working against me. I realized if I wanted to gain some ground for myself and for God's purpose with my life, I was going to have to not be victim to such things. I had to learn to become the "no" girl; I had to start telling people "no." First, I practiced with small nos—the simple and straightforward no's. No, I cannot have that done by Thursday. No, I can't promise to do all that extra stuff when I know I will be working a lot this week. No, I won't try to tackle that huge project by myself.

Then I had to go for bigger no's. I had to get proficient at the bigger, deeper, widespread no's. No, I'm not going to say yes to you because I really have no intention of doing that or making your request a priority. This was a big eye opener for me, because I had grown used to trying to make everyone happy and trying and failing to meet everyone's request. I literally had to drag the word "no" kicking and screaming into my vocabulary. What it showed me was that I was terrible about following through with making things a priority when I said I would. Ouch, this was very painful to see that I was failing miserably at everything from being on time, to not doing what I said I'd do. I was then having to cancel things at the last minute and hide in shame because I was too people-pleasey to say no in the first place. This was really costly! I did not take myself seriously and could not expect anyone else to take me seriously either.

Then came bigger and weightier no's; no's that spanned whole relationships. No, I cannot be responsible for your happiness. No, I won't continue to make up for your irresponsibility. No, I will not stay in a relationship where you are trying to guilt me into thinking it's often my fault. No, I will not interact with you while you are speaking or acting disrespectfully.

Saying "no" as a part of having healthy boundaries created some waves, but I was committed to letting the waves do their thing and reach wherever they will. The waves actually washed out a lot of bad and/or useless stuff from my life. The process was very uncomfortable, but the resulting freedom and self-control was priceless! Some relationships dissolved and in those instances it was for the better. Many relationships improved drastically, though, as people began to learn to respect the boundaries I'd set and adjusted and grew with me. It is a wonderful phenomenon that the waves created by building healthy boundaries can wash away some needless things from our lives.

But let your speech be, 'Yes, yes,' or 'No, no,'
and whatever is more than this is of the wicked one.
Matthew 5:37

Read any of the Cloud and Townsend books on *Boundaries*. When you do open your mouth, be honest; but don't feel you have to talk about everything to everybody. Not all people are safe or trustworthy. Sometimes you still have to be with them, work with them, and interact with them. We do the best we can to do the job well, but we don't have to have friendships with coworkers or anyone else. You can treat someone with love, respect, and dignity without hanging out or sharing secrets with him/her.

Let your conversation be always full of grace, seasoned with salt,
so that you may know how to answer everyone.
Colossians 4:6

Allow for the best possible outcome, and add truth wherever you can. This can be easy with those you like and with whom you get along. It can be more challenging with those you don't. Nonetheless, you can be honest and genuine without being ugly. You can have good boundaries and still answer. You can also have wisdom about when not to answer.

WHEN PEOPLE DON'T LIKE US

Sometimes time, work, and prayer will turn an apparent enemy into a friend, or the reverse. Other times, it's just good to move on. Remember, some people are just not going to like us. We are not for everybody. When we run into people who don't like us, we need to stay keenly attuned to from where we are drawing our value. Honest self-examination may tell us if we are deriving value from a relationship motive that is selfish, not helpful, or not from God.

We don't have to try to understand it all. Just move on and do your thing.

Some people will never like you because your spirit irritates their demons.
DENZEL WASHINGTON

MOVING ON

We become excellent people to be in a relationship with when we become people of character who honor our word and have healthy boundaries. Then something even more wonderful happens. Relationships often improve exponentially. When we offer integrity, solid character, genuine care and love to others, it has a ripple effect in our lives as well as those with whom we are in relationship. The quality of our relationships becomes more buoyant and rises above where they used to be. Everything becomes richer and better.

Questions to ponder about relating: To what things am I willing to say no, that will enable me to be unencumbered to say my big yeses?

In what ways can I move toward being a person who fulfills my commitments, keeps my promises and honors my word?

How can I be bolder and less fearful about being honest with myself and others and let go of the outcome?

PRAYER

Father, thank You that You are the perfect example of someone who always keeps His promises and always keeps His Word. Thank You for helping us enjoy and experience the richness of what You intended relationships to be. Thank You for refining us and growing us in Your wisdom and understanding about when to say "yes," when to say "no," and how to honor our commitments to You, one another and ourselves. Thank You for helping us to be discerning about proper boundaries, how to interact, and how to let things go when we should. Thank You for bringing health and healing to our relationships. Help us to forgive others; help us to be forgiving of ourselves; and thank You for helping us to always treat others as we would want to be treated. Thank You for all these things, in the name of Your Son Jesus Christ.

CHAPTER EIGHT

THE SAFETY OF A SHARK CAGE

In this chapter, I will describe what I call the Shark Cage Analogy of a "racket" and in the next chapter, *The Dangers of a Shark Cage*, I will give specific examples from my own life.

So, what is a shark cage? A shark cage (or shark-proof cage), according to Wikipedia, is:

> *A shark proof cage is an extremely strong, metal cage used by a scuba diver to safely examine dangerous types of sharks up close. This can include various species of shark, but the most commonly observed within the confines of a cage are the great white shark and the bull shark, which are both known to be aggressive at times. Shark proof cages are built to withstand being rammed at high velocities, and be able to protect the user from massive force from attacks. Cages can provide a visual*

and tactile deterrent to sharks. Cage-diving allows people to closely monitor sharks, and sometimes interact with them.

A shark cage allows you to exist in a potentially dangerous situation with a greatly decreased risk of being eaten or injured by large, toothy, dangerous creatures. The cage is initially, constructed to serve as a temporary defense mechanism. During a time of impending danger (e.g., abuse, hardship, loss, tragedy, rejection, abandonment, or any other number of traumatic situations), we sometimes suffer injuries or the threat of injuries, which compels us to respond by setting up defense mechanisms to protect ourselves. It's only natural. We all do it.

The idea of keeping our defense mechanism going too long, or staying in our shark cage unnecessarily, is similar to running a "racket". A racket, in its raw concept, I've heard described, is a fraudulent cover of protection or something that is fabricated to conceal or protect something else, much like a benign-looking storefront in Prohibition days. I learned about rackets in a powerful training called "Breakthrough". Humans can tend to develop such rackets in our lives in an effort to "protect" ourselves. These are usually highly structured, firmly reinforced ways of trying to avoid repeat injuries. A shark cage is useful only while there are sharks around, protecting us for a very short and specific time. It is not usually helpful for living the rest of life, though, after the original danger is gone. This shark cage analogy comes with the analogous components of a racket: the complaint, the resulting behavior, the payoffs, and finally the costs.

It all starts as a simple complaint. We were unduly threatened, unjustly harmed, unfairly treated, rejected as unworthy of a relationship, or worse. Over time, we notice recurring ways we are treated unjustly or unfairly; and the complaint becomes more and more supported by similar occasions of the offense; the evidence piles up. Thank goodness for the protection of the shark cage. I can use what I have to build the perfect shark cage. This leads to the next part, the resulting behavior.

I hide, withdraw, shut down, quit trusting, and quit taking risks altogether. I withdraw into my shark cage. I am not really reachable inside the protective boundaries of the bars. I do not have to really show up in a big way to expose myself or help others be who they really are. I can play small. After all, I've been hurt. Who can expect more from me?

We unknowingly or subconsciously use the no-longer-needed equipment as if it were vital to our survival in our present circumstances. The shark cage really did protect me from those sharks. However, now that I am back on the boat (or getting on with life), I somehow manage to unconsciously stay in the cage longer than I need to…a lot longer. The craftsmanship and sturdiness of the cage served me then, so won't it come in handy still? In fact, I subconsciously assume it is necessary for life. I've gotten pretty used to the idea that I am safe inside it and would feel vulnerable, almost naked, if those bars are not surrounding me. Sadly, by running these rackets, we greatly limit ourselves from being fully genuine in relationships and situations.

I can see just fine between the bars of my cage—so much so that I focus right past them like they aren't even there—much like when I focus my camera past the chain-link fence to get a great picture of an animal at the zoo. When I need to reach out to grab something or someone, I can fit my hands and arms out and not even realize I'm actually reaching out through the set of bars. Everything is just fine. I can "selectively" interact with people just as I did with those sharks back there, without 'getting hurt.'

Back on land, long after the close call with the sharks and the boat ride back, I walk step by step with my feet touching the ground as they always have, with the exception that I haven't even realized I've slightly adjusted my stride to step between the bars of the cage that I'm dragging along. I haven't really noticed that I'm dragging this well-made, structurally sound, heavy piece of equipment around with me. I've unknowingly gotten used to its mass and cumbersomeness. Life seems a bit harder these days, but, hey, I'm getting stronger with more resistance in life. What doesn't kill me makes me stronger, right? Besides, life is generally similar to the way it's always been. I see, talk, interact, listen to music, enjoy some hobbies, and generally go about business as usual.

There are no small numbers of payoffs for unconsciously maintaining my position in this shark cage. I felt justified in maintaining my distance and protection from the threats to which I've been exposed. I was at risk of being attacked and deserved to be protected. I've been bitten before and know how badly it hurts and the serious, even life-threatening, injuries it can cause. I'll not allow others to harm me the way they once did or could have. Others are dangerous, and I must refrain from interacting with them too closely.

I cannot be exposed. I cannot be vulnerable. I deserve to feel safe. Most people seem to treat me normally; and few seem to notice that I am still within the confines of my protection that I needed a while back with those sharks. Besides, I've unknowingly gotten used to it, so much so that other folks have, too. Some people even recognize me for my protectiveness (cage). Others, I think, avoid messing with me because I'm somewhat untouchable. After all, shark cages can be, as the definition above mentioned, "a visual and tactile deterrent to sharks." Those sharks will not be able to engage with me as they might like. In fact, not many other things will either. I get to feel justified in living this way because I've been hurt before. I've been threatened by the sharks of life too many times.

After a long while, I've not noticed that I've incurred some costs for allowing myself to stay in this shark cage. The lasting tragedy is that we all spend so much time constructing and reinforcing these shark cages (rackets) that we don't leave them behind after the impending danger is gone. When I am in it, it seems so easy to stay in it—we get accustomed to its comfortably-protective structure.

Upon exposing this racket and after taking a long, close look at what was happening to my life since being in the cage, I've been able to see that the perceived protection I was getting was costing me much more than I ever thought. Not only was I dragging around the unimaginable weight of an old situation, but I had built up a tolerance for it—even thought I needed it—and couldn't be without it. It had become part of me.

It wasn't!

The shark cage (or racket) was not only NOT a part of me, but it also stood between me and the genuine enjoyment of real life. I had been so worried about being protected from sharks that my own friends and loved ones couldn't even get close to me or I to them. I wasn't able to move through life with the agility I would have wanted and to be in close and loving relationships. I missed out on this closeness to people because I could go only where my cage could fit.

That shark cage, my old defense mechanism, now figuratively sits covered with dust in the garage. I've made the choice to come out of it; now it no longer encapsulates or hinders me. Sure, every once in a while it calls to me; and I am tempted to get back in. However, it no longer has any power over me. I know that real power, genuinely flourishing relationships, and a truly joy-filled life are all outside of the cage.

What has served as your shark cage?

What is it that you'd be willing to lay aside so that you can experience deeper, richer, more genuine relationships?

What is it, that, if you choose to forgive it, would set you free?

Stay tuned and I'll walk you through one of my shark cages.

PRAYER

Father, teach me about my heart; help me understand the ways I've let lies build up and be used against me and my fulfilling my Purpose in You. Forgive me for the ways I've held onto hurts and resentments all the while foregoing the great level of freedom You've already made available for me. Thank You for Your tender, loving kindness, Your great mercies that are new every morning, and Your ever-covering grace. Help me to see my temporary defense mechanisms for what they are, and help me to not cling to them for safety. You are my safety! Show me what it's like to be genuinely and fearlessly open and loving to You, myself, and others. Help me to live and love courageously, for You are my protector, my defender, my vindicator, and my safe place. Thank You for all of these things in the name of Your Son Jesus Christ.

CHAPTER NINE

THE DANGER OF A SHARK CAGE

To give you some additional helpful information on the shark cage (racket) scenario, I want to share with you one of the shark cages I finally dealt with that transformed my life. I'm going to briskly walk you through some of my old pain to show you how this racket, or shark cage, works.

The transforming work is becoming aware of it, recognizing it for what it is (a system of thought) and refusing to stay in or get back in it.

Rackets:

It was quite an eye-opener to see how these thought/behavior systems work in helping or hurting relationships and productivity. In the book called *The Three Laws of Performance*, Steve Zaffron and Dave Logan write, "Becoming aware of rackets—and taking responsibility for them—is one of the most important aspects in elevating performance."

So, I'm going to give you the layout of one of my ugliest and most painful rackets. It's big and it runs deep; and to this day it tries to lure me back in from time to time. It's nothing to be afraid of, though, as you will see. It is a system of thinking. That means that I am at any time able to derail it with truth and awareness.

Let's take a look.

As mentioned in the last chapter, there are four parts to the racket: The Complaint, The Behavior, the Pay-Offs, and the Costs.

Before I continue, I want to give a qualifying disclaimer. It may seem I'm being cavalier about the events of my life, but I can do so from a place of healing. There were times I hurt so deeply I couldn't find the words to describe it. These old wounds have been healed by God's love, my loving connections with some people, time and growth, and my consistent decision to let God make me whole in all aspects. When God provides healing, it is good and it is complete. Although you can sometimes see evidence of a scar, the pain goes away and function is restored.

Let's dive into the complaint.

My complaint: I'm not worth sticking around for.

Please keep in mind that I'm baring the raw, distilled complaint. The truth is that it is a lie; and it's an ugly one at that. I know it is a lie, and most people would agree that it is a lie. Although the complaint is not true, I inadvertently behaved as if it were. I can produce plenty of evidence that proves I was loved and I was and am worth sticking around for. However, in some important areas of my life, I was not bearing the good results.

Just weeks after my twelfth birthday, my mother passed away. It was a nightmare that had become reality. She had struggled with cancer and the harsh results of treatments for over six years. She had such a hard time for so many years that I couldn't blame her if she'd lost her will to fight. A part of me was relieved that she was not suffering anymore. Nonetheless, we were without her this side of heaven; and I was suffering terribly without her. It was so incredibly hard for so long.

Decades later I learned that grieving the loss of someone close to you is somehow processed emotionally in a similar way to rejection. Hence, I viewed my mom's passing as a rejection of me, which spurred my thoughts of not being worth sticking around for. Although I knew this was not true, I subconsciously behaved as if it were. As other bad things that resembled this rejection and pain happened to me, I compiled a heap of evidence to support this awful lie. Anything in life that vaguely resembled this form of hurt got added to the list. The evidence began to accumulate. Notice that the complaint is able to be reinforced even years afterward by new supporting pieces of evidence that run along with the same old theme. I used these new incidences to bolster the old story.

My big brother had moved out of the house a few years before mom died. In the tender and sad weeks and months after my mom's passing, he stopped over for a visit here and there. I was so happy to see him every time he walked through the door. He often visited when I was home alone after school while my dad was still at work. My brother talked with me for a bit, got this mail, and left. His infrequent visits didn't last that long, as he was busy with work and his girlfriend. We were in entirely different stages of life. I craved his attention and company and was crushed every time he left. I'm sure he had no idea how his leaving inadvertently aided the case of rejection against me.

In addition, I was not the most popular kid in school. I was overweight for much of my childhood (and much of my adulthood), was often teased, was picked last for games in gym class, and did not date any prom kings or star athletes in school. Later, I had a long-term boyfriend who dumped me. In my early thirties, an ex-boyfriend, who was still a close friend, passed away unexpectedly. We had been emotionally close for years, and I felt like I had been widowed after his passing. I was traumatized for such a long time. It took me years to heal and feel "normal" again.

After another couple of years, I developed a crush on one of my coworkers. Although we were not dating, I loved him dearly and wanted to be with him. He died tragically in a terrible accident; and I, again, felt like I had been widowed. In my late 30s I had a few more losses of close friends, and in my early 40s, a loss of a really close friend who was also becoming a would-be boyfriend; these really sent me reeling. I had some deep and lengthy emotional connections to people who had passed away abruptly or expectedly after sickness. It seemed like a year or two after I'd recovered emotionally from one loss, I was facing another. For a few intense years, I was completely overwhelmed with grief. I was sick and tired of feeling abandoned and continually steeped in grief.

My family and friends witnessed my grief during these back-to-back losses but didn't know how to comfort me or help me move on. They did everything they knew to do, but I found it safer just to stay home and have a glass of wine…or three.

Despite my ongoing grief, my life was not all doom and gloom. I was not alone; I had an interesting and rewarding career, good friends and family… and I had God. People everywhere fight hard battles every day. I am simply painting the picture of the pattern that started to emerge for me. The story playing in my head about myself was: I'm not worth sticking around for.

The Behavior: As a result of my complaint, I was leery of relationships. I expected people to eventually leave me, so I did not want to get too attached to them. Instead of going out with friends and staying active and involved in social activities like someone who was hopeful for a good future, I thought it was just safer to stay home and drink wine. I especially avoided any romantic relationship because I feared the person would die, as some of the others I was close with had. Yes, I know most people die at some point in the twilight years of their lives; but I was getting really tired of death surrounding my current age group, especially that of a few men I was very emotionally close to. Sadly, I began to see men as people who would just end up leaving me, instead of potential dating partners. I didn't want to be an ex-girlfriend or a widow. Although I was not married to any of these people, a few of these losses were men I was emotionally close to and had hoped would have been dating partners. I realize now how sad my thought process had become. I had helped plan too many memorial services and was shying away from the possibility of any more.

I shut down any possibilities for romantic relationships. Although I was a person who was intrinsically friendly, social, and outgoing, I fled from any situation where I could possibly be asked out on a date. A side effect was that I had become comfortable with being about 40 pounds overweight and, therefore, invisible to many men. If I stayed home alone or watched movies with my sister, there were zero possibilities of my being asked out on a date. Who would want a date anyway? It could mean just another funeral to plan. No way.

Unfortunately, any loss of life around me was immediately heaped onto the already huge pile of evidence that supported my belief that I was not worth sticking around for. I further justified my singlehood by reminding myself I had been single almost all of my adult life and got along "just fine."

Over the years, I watched many of my friends and peers date, get married, and have babies. Although I was happy for them, I was resigned to the idea that all of these happy life events were for other people, and I was just a helpful bystander. I also watched many other friends and peers get their hearts broken. In these situations, I rejoiced that I had virtually no chance of having my heart broken in this way. I began to think I was soaring above this type of heartbreak. When I thought I was soaring, I had really been "sore-ing."

This leads right into the Payoffs.

My rising above heartbreak allowed me to feel invincible to life's dating and psychological knockdowns. I felt justified in staying emotionally secluded. I began to pity my poor friends who would get the run around by becoming intimate too quickly, getting their hopes up that a relationship or person might be the right one (or at least headed in the right direction), and then skidding into yet another heartbreak. It seemed like a hopeless cycle, and I wanted no part of anything like it. No thanks. I began to feel wiser than those people who were in the romantic relationship arena getting their butts kicked. I was starting to feel somewhat superior to them. Oh, that sounds ugly.

My clarifying moment occurred while I was talking to a close friend on the phone. She was telling me about one of her recent dating experiences. She had again been a little too physically intimate (so I thought, but I guess I was always thinking that because, hey, I was a virgin waiting for marriage and everyone else should be too; shame on them!) and had gotten hurt when her date didn't contact her again. She was really upset. She thought he was going to be a keeper. She was pouring out the painful details to me as I listened. As I was "consoling" her, I caught a glimpse of myself in the mirror across from my dining room table. I saw myself roll my eyes at her current emotional derailing event. I had done enough reading about interpersonal behavior to know that eye-rolling was sometimes a sign of contempt.

Ouch. Was that really me "contempting" her? As she talked on, I studied myself in that mirror. Instead of seeing compassion and friendship, I saw superiority and disgust. Instead of kindness, I saw judgment. Instead of humility, I saw pride. Wow, was it ugly! I had always considered myself a true, kind and loving friend; but my mirror was showing a different side of me. It was a painful awakening. I had played right into the idea that I had been a victim and felt I was justified in everything I did or didn't do regarding this area of life.

In light of these ugly payoffs, I was able to take a realistic assessment of the costs.

THE COSTS

Assessing the costs that this racket was having on me was the big turning point.

Here's the summary of my cost list.

First, this was costing me a romantic relationship leading to marriage. (Oh my gosh! I was keeping myself from this!) In the beginning it involved many factors; but by feeling justified to stay in the shark cage, I was refusing for the last decade or so to be open to the possibility of romantic love in my life. Wow!

Second, this was costing my future husband a chance to even get to know me. When I considered that keeping myself closed off was also depriving my future husband of his would-be wife (and a potentially awesome one at that!), I could hardly swallow that pill. This suddenly got a lot bigger than just me.

This was also costing me genuine intimacy in friendships. That glance in the mirror was a tell-tale. After all, how could I be a true friend while I was rolling my condescending eyes at another's mistakes and heartaches? This was definitely not even in the ballpark of treating others as I would want to be treated; so another intrinsic cost was that I was compromising my character in friendships as well. I was not being a genuine friend, so how could I realistically expect to have genuine loving and life-giving connections?

These costs were adding up to a price I was unwilling to pay. Ever. Not even on time-installments. I simply could not afford it.

Immediately, when adding up these costs, the chains started to fall off. I swung open the shark cage door, took a step forward, and firmly placed my feet outside. I closed the door behind me and pushed the cage aside.

At once, I was free…and fully alive.

Ah, transformation. Sometimes it is simply the wisdom of the truth that sets us free. I was so grateful to learn how to look at myself honestly and consider that I had built up systems of thought that were working against my heart's desires and purposes. It was a very hard lesson, but I would not want to unlearn it.

Was it scary? Yes.

Was it worth it? Yes. Every day.

Did I know I was probably going to experience emotional hurt? Gulp,…yes.

Did I get hurt? You bet!

Have I experienced sadness and heartache since then? Yes.

Am I willing to really live anyway ? Yes.

I came to the realization that I'd rather be at risk of experiencing some emotional pain associated with the joy of connection than in the confines of the "safer" loneliness of numb isolation.

Dear ones, life has hurts no matter what. It might as well be while you are free and not in a shark cage of emotional isolation.

What thought system are you willing to step outside of to live free?

What will no longer stop you from being a fully genuine and life-giving part of a relationship?

What connections in your life will be better because you choose to bring your full and free self to the relationship?

The Man in the Arena

by Theodore Roosevelt

> It is not the critic who counts; not the man who points out how the strong man stumbles, or where the doer of deeds could have done them better. The credit belongs to the man who is actually in the arena, whose face is marred by dust and sweat and blood; who strives valiantly; who errs, who comes short again and again, because there is no effort without error and shortcoming; but who does actually strive to do the deeds; who knows great enthusiasms, the great devotions; who spends himself in a worthy cause; who at the best knows in the end the triumph of high achievement, and who at the worst, if he fails, at least fails while daring greatly, so that his place shall never be with those cold and

timid souls who neither know victory nor defeat.

Lets' get into the arena of life where we can make a difference and fully live.

PRAYER

Father, thank You for Your truth that sets us free! Thank You that You have purchased true freedom for us, making us Your sons and daughters. Thank You that we are free agents of Your Kingdom, able to call on You, our Mighty God, from Your Throne room of grace. Thank You that we are no longer prisoners of fear. We have been bought with the blood of Jesus Christ and are free. Thank You that we can live unencumbered by lies and systems of thought that would otherwise entangle us. We can choose to walk in the freedom You've already provided for us. We can know that You'll be there to help us when we hurt, lift our chins when we are downcast, comfort us when we need, and strengthen us for any occasion. Help us to not shy away from our callings. Help us to walk boldly into our destinies and our purposes to which You've called us! Above all, we ask that You bring about Your will in our lives! We thank You for all of these things, in the name of Your Son Jesus Christ.

CHAPTER TEN

DON'T GIVE UP THE SHIP

On the bridge of one ship I worked on, wedged between some of the officers' training manuals, was a small blue flag with white letters that read, "DON'T GIVE UP THE SHIP."

It struck me as extremely profound, and it seemed to apply to nearly everything. The ship could be the actual ship I was on. Don't give it up! The ship could also represent me, you, us, our destinies, our families, our businesses, or whatever entity on which we are literally or figuratively sailing through life. Whatever we are sailing on, it is NOT to be given up.

In the last 15 years or so I've accumulated more than 1,500 sea days. Some people might say I'm pretty salty, but I'm just a scientist who often works at sea conducting research surveys on marine wildlife. While underway, we practice lots of drills: fire drills, general emergency drills, abandon ship drills, man overboard drills, and occasionally even terrorism drills, etc. However, one of the scariest drills that I've practiced was a pirate drill. And by pirate I don't mean the swanky Captain Jack Sparrow kind of pirate. I mean the really bad pirates. I mean the ones who board ships and forcefully take over the mission and purpose of the ship and its cargo. Granted, we were at a lower risk because we were on a science mission and didn't really have any equipment or cargo that pirates would want; nevertheless, we had to train for such emergencies.

Training included learning passwords and phrases to communicate with each other without the intruder's knowledge, how to get to safe places, and how and when to lock or open certain areas. The first and basic component of response, though, was simply being aware of the presence of an intruder. Amidst the many procedures and instructions to follow, initial awareness was key to an effective response.

Just as we don't want anyone to physically take over control, we don't want certain undesirable thoughts to hijack our purpose. Don't let thoughts or systems of thought take over your ship. As I described in the previous chapter, I had let my system of thought, my racket or shark cage, determine whether or not I could be open to a loving, romantic relationship. That system of thought, like so many others, was one that kept me in a hiding, victim sort of mentality where I had shied away from really living. We are ultimately the choosers, the decision makers, and the ones with the final say of what we believe and on what we will act. It is when we take responsibility for our responses to our thoughts that we become free agents. Let's not turn our controls over to those thoughts.

Many thoughts "fly" through our minds, whipping around and sometimes sticking for a while. Nonetheless, we ultimately choose what thoughts we allow to linger. We can give a thought a seat and have it stay, or we can make sure it leaves so that it does not become a part of us.

We demolish arguments and every pretension that sets itself up against the knowledge of God, and we take captive every thought to make it obedient to Christ.
2 Corinthians 10:5

One day I was spending time with God and trying to wrap my head around this verse. How could this verse help me manage thoughts? What exactly am I to do to "take captive every thought?"

The imagery that began to form for me was a baseball analogy. Sometimes a ball, or a thought, comes flying out of nowhere at us; and we either catch it, dodge it, or get hit by it.

Let's say the scenario is that we catch it—we take it into our control for observation. And then the decision about what to do with it is the "take all thoughts captive part." Sometimes it's very obvious where the thought came from. If it's a thought that lines up with God's Word and is helpful and good and obvious it's a good thought, then we keep it. Put it in our satchel.

For most folks, if it's clearly a bad thought, like "I should go rob a bank!" it's obviously not the kind of thought we want. W e don't keep it; we throw it or bat it out of there as quickly as possible. Done.

If it is a thought we are unsure of, we take the thought, like a baseball in our hand, and lift it up to the Lord, asking , "Okay, Lord, what shall I do with this one?" If He helps us understand it is a bad, unhelpful thought and something that could be used to hold us captive, then we get rid of it. Knock it out of the park, so to speak. If a similar thought keeps coming, we continue to knock it out of the park as many times as needed. My favorite way to think about it is to throw the ball up, swing the bat, make contact, and send it out of the park, way out past the bleachers, so it's no longer in the ballpark.

If it's not obvious where the thought is from or what we should do with it, or if the answer is unclear, we wait for an answer from the Lord. Sometimes, if the answer does not come immediately, we toss the thought back and forth with our teammates. Many of them can echo the Lord's voice in our lives and can help us discern what to do. Be careful, though, to let the Lord have the final say. People are people. Although they may be our brothers and sisters in Christ, they are still not the final say. The final say belongs to the Lord. Seek Him first and His wisdom. The right answer will not contradict His word or His character.

We have the final say of whom we will obey. It is up to us to give that say to the Lord.

Will we obey the thoughts or will we obey the Lord?

What thoughts or systems of thoughts are you willing to take to the Lord for examination?

What freedoms await if you choose to take your thoughts captive into the obedience of Christ?

PRAYER

Father, I thank You that You've paved the way for our freedom, that we can take our thoughts captive into the obedience of Christ so that we do not have to stay imprisoned in those thoughts or systems of thoughts any longer. Help us to see through the stories and lies that stand against us becoming who You meant us to be. Thank You for helping us, Father, by bringing about Your will for us and our lives. Help us to boldly challenge thoughts and put them in their proper place. Help us to agree with thoughts that align with Your truth and disagree with or reject any thoughts that oppose Your heart and Your will for us. Thank You for helping us to 'Never Give Up the Ship!' in the name of Your Son Jesus Christ.

CHAPTER ELEVEN

SEA KELP

SEEK HELP!

Whales are not meant to drag around fishing gear. They are large and powerful creatures, but they are designed to be free of external burdens. Even in their weightless environment, a seemingly small entanglement can cause some serious hindrances. Over time, if they are not removed, these hindrances can cause long-term stress, chronic problems, and affect the individual's ability to thrive. Whales are meant to travel, eat, form social bonds with other whales, and work together to have and raise strong, healthy, well-adjusted baby whales.

Dragging emotional burdens around weighs down our minds and our hearts. Like gear that is dragging on a whale, these things are energetically expensive; and they cut into our lives. We know how this is. For example, when I am going through a trying time with a family member or friend, I find it hard to concentrate on work, or fun, or anything else. Case in point, just now, as I am reworking this chapter, I had a tense conversation with my very closest friend. We'd had a disagreement or breach in trust a couple days ago, and there were some pretty weighty words and hurts exchanged. In each post-argument conversation, we've been more understanding of one another; and there is some emerging hope for healing. It is not yet complete, and there are no guarantees. Although we are closer to resolving things than we were, the ordeal is taxing on my heart, upsetting to my stomach, and taking up a lot of my mental bandwidth. It's taking effort and time to make the needed repairs and rebuild trust.

As a result of this emotional burden, I had to read the previous paragraph's "Dragging emotional burdens around..." first sentence about six times before I was able to refocus my attention onto editing this chapter. Of course, I had a bit of a laugh at the ridiculous irony of my emotional burden inhibiting my ability to understand what I read in this very chapter. The even funnier part is that I had been making suggested corrections by one of my editors, and she had included a comment about needing to include a personal example of how emotional burdens cause hindrances. Here was the very example I needed that was distracting me from this very task. Like dragging unwanted gear, or clumsily trying to swim through an underwater forest of seaweed, emotional burdens can cause a lot of drag in our lives. That is why it's so important to remove what we can and deal with the rest so we are not hindered from living our fullest, most purposeful lives.

When an emotional burden is resolved, you can feel the dragging weight break away. It is then easier to move forward unencumbered.

Unforgiveness leads to many problems. Like being entangled in a forest of kelp, unforgiveness traps us in unnecessary places, limiting our growth and providing a foothold for evil. I've found that the start of my problems or a whole series of problems often stems from unforgiveness. Forgiveness, the remedy, is both a decision and a lifelong commitment. It is also an event and an ongoing process, like repeatedly netting leaves out of a pool as they continue to fall in or scraping off the barnacles and other unwanted growth from the hull of a boat to avoid unwanted drag. You have to be committed to maintaining the forgiveness that you've declared and achieved. When bitter temptations try to lead you astray, stay the course; and don't buy into the tired old lie that you are still a victim. More importantly, don't fall into a romance with revenge.

Do not envy a violent man or choose any of his ways,
for the LORD detests a perverse man but takes the upright into his confidence.
Proverbs 3:31-32

I love this verse because I feel it's like God saying, "You don't have to exact justice here; don't lower yourself to the level of evil so that you don't become like them. I detest them like you do and I will handle it for good; it will be complete and final, a better job than you can do. You can just wait in confidence, because I've got this. Follow me, trust me, and I'll take you under my arm; I'll pull you close to my voice, tell you what you need to know, and lead you through this."

Forgiveness is one of the most important gifts we can give ourselves and others. It means realizing that we are not enchained by the wrongs done to us. Learn the skill of forgiving. Learn it well. Practice it daily. The Bible commands us to forgive. When we abide by this commandment, we are rewarded in so many ways. We have been forgiven much, and so we are commanded to forgive also. Other people cannot pay us back for the wrongs they have inflicted (intentionally or unintentionally). The sooner we give up the idea we can be compensated by them for our losses, the freer we will be. Remember that there is a distinction between trust and forgiveness. Forgiveness means maintaining your freedom despite the offense. Jesus paid the price for our freedom. Let's enjoy it.

God is truly the only one who can compensate for the damages. Besides temporary monetary settlements people sometimes receive when things go wrong, God is really the only one who can make amends over the long term. Let God make you whole again. He's the only one who can really do it. Looking back, I've not once said to myself, "I'm so glad I remained bitter about that thing for so long!"

If the same thinking and resources we've been using haven't brought the desired results, then maybe we need new information, ideas, concepts, or tools to solve our issues.

We cannot solve our problems with the same thinking we used when we created them.
ALBERT EINSTEIN

Get wisdom, get understanding; do not forget my words or turn away from them.
Proverbs 4:5

If you need therapy or counseling, get it. Get the help you need.

We have been given the tools to be free from entanglements. Unforgiveness, along with worry, fear, and shame, keeps us from living the way God intended us to live. Let's make it a priority to deal with some of these issues so we may live unhindered and free. Let's deal with what we need to deal with.

The Bible says *there is nothing new under the sun* (Ecclesiastes 1:9). Chances are what you are dealing with has been dealt with before. Find those who can help you.

If counseling or coaching might help in your struggles, take advantage of them. If you are living a life that is not quite what you believe you are called to, check into this. Do not dismiss the possibility of getting some help. Old hurts, unforgiveness, and shame-based thoughts are all primary reasons many of us miss out on fulfilling a portion of, or all of, our destinies. Sometimes there are spiritual influences going on as well that we need to deal with and that may require prayer or deliverance. Get the help you need. Ask God to help you find it.

Coaching can also be helpful. Coaching involves working with someone who can help you see around your own blind spots; he or she can perhaps help you see yourself and your situations differently, which can create some very positive changes in specific or general areas of your life. I have worked with a coach for several years and have only great things to say about it. It has enabled me to free myself from some of my old entanglements and have more of an impact on the world that I desire for God and for myself. In essence, I feel better equipped to love people (including myself) and am less apt to let some of the same old things hinder me from being my best version of myself.

Don't wait for something better. Create something better.

PRAYER

Father, help us to become disentangled and free from all that has ensnared us or threatens to ensnare us. Lead us to the help we need. Lead us to those who can help us, support us, or connect us to those who can. Father, thank You that we are Your children, bought with the highest price of Jesus Christ's sacrifice. We belong to You, and Satan has no right to us nor power over us. We ask for freedom under the authority of Jesus Christ from all evil purposes. Help us to be filled with Your gift of the holy spirit, and able to hear Your voice and follow Your lead. Thank You for giving us courage to see what about ourselves is a hindrance to us and preventing us from fulfilling our destinies. Help us to remove all of these entanglements, and help us to grow and mature in You. Thank You for helping us to become free to fulfill Your purposes for us and enjoy all the freedom and goodness You have for us. We rejoice in You, Father, and we thank You for all these things in the name of Your Son Jesus Christ.

CHAPTER TWELVE

USE TELL-TALES

What is working well in your life?

And what is not working well in your life?

Are there relationships that, if improved even a little, would make life easier or better?

I've found taking ownership and making improvements on my end of things started a positive shift in my life. Sometimes even just adjusting my part or the way I contribute to a relationship improves the way we both relate, thereby impacting the whole relationship. Let's make it a goal to own 100% of our 50% share in each of our relationships.

One of the simplest ways to do this is to receive and use honest feedback. Use tell-tale signs, or tell-tales.

Let's say you are sailing a sailboat. You want to ensure you are maximizing the use of the wind to get you from Point A to Point B. From the helm looking up on the sail, you can see a set of tell-tales. They are usually little ribbons, sometimes one on either side of a sail, that indicate how the wind and sail interact. Depending on the effect of the wind on the angle of the sail, the tell-tales will be hanging loosely, streaming behind horizontally, or fluttering about. The sailor can look up at the tell-tales and trim (adjust) the sail to maximize the effect of the wind. If, for instance, considering the boat's heading and wind direction, the sail is adjusted too loosely, the windward tell-tale will hang loosely; and the sail will be luffing or not catching all of the available wind. The result is the boat won't make good headway. If the sail is drawn in too tightly, the tell-tale will be flailing about wildly, meaning too much of the available wind is having an overbearing effect on the sail, causing drag instead of push. Again, the result is the boat won't make good headway. If the tell-tale is streaming back steadily in a horizontal line, the wind's effect on the sail is just about perfect—Goldilocks—not too hard, not too soft, but just right—making GREAT headway.

Using tell-tales is simply taking advantage of instant feedback. Feedback is wonderful for gauging how to proceed or deciding what adjustments can be made to maximize advancement in any number of things.

BLIND SPOTS

What about in relationships? Why should we tune in to feedback? We should do so because it's really helpful. In fact, for certain purposes, we should seek feedback. We all have blind spots. We all have areas in our lives where we are missing the mark, often unknowingly, in our relationships.

For instance, how many times have we intended one thing by what we say, do, or don't do, but the impact our action or inaction has on another results in something that was not at all what we intended. If we have a pattern of being misunderstood, maybe we owe it to ourselves and others to take another look at how we are perceived. In relationships, most of us would do whatever we can to close the gap between our intent and the impact it has on others. The best part is it's not hard; and in many cases it's as simple as asking and listening—seeking feedback in safe relationships.

Humans have no shortage of tell-tale tools or ways to get feedback. When I first learned of the intent/impact gap a few years ago—yes, I'd probably been abusing it all my life, and it was exhausting—I desperately wanted to close that gap. I asked a mentor how he would suggest I do so, and he simply answered, "Just ask people!" How profoundly simple.

I found myself slightly aggravated with that answer but only because it seemed too easy. It was a little unnerving to think about asking my friends such a thing and then terrifying to think I may have to eat a big slice of humble pie when I heard their answers. What if I didn't like or agree with their answers? Well, I was asking for their answers—not mine. Or worse, what if what they told me was a terrible thing about myself that I already suspected was there? What a nightmare! People might already know to be true what I feared about myself? This was indeed scary territory.

Additionally, I may have to adjust my ways of relating after hearing their responses, and that, too, was a scary thought! Did I really want to know? Suddenly the gravity and fear of what I might learn about myself crept in. As I gave myself a little time to settle into my decision—I really did want to know how I come across in relationships—the method of how to ask for it became a little clearer.

JUST DIVE IN

With my scientific background, I could not resist diving into the experiment. I drafted a few simple questions in an email to my three closest, most honest, and trustworthy friends.

Hi, I am currently working on a self-improvement project; and I desire some honest feedback about how I relate to you in our friendship. Brutally honest answers will be most helpful to me. I am asking for this because I value your opinion and genuinely want to know how I come across and how it may vary from how I think I come across. Please don't hold back—I am really asking for it.

How long have we known each other?

Please list three areas where you feel I do well in our friendship.

Please list three (or more) areas where you feel I miss the mark.

Thanks for your honesty and candor.

I also called to inform them I'd be sending this request and to encourage them in three things: to give completely honest answers, not to worry about hurting my feelings because I very much wanted to know, and that I would not harbor ill feelings about any seemingly negative feedback. It was all JUST feedback. I was wanting and needing any and all information; and I was considering it all helpful to me because it was coming from them – my trusted, respected and loved inner circle.

Wounds from a friend can be trusted, but an enemy multiplies kisses.

Proverbs 27:6

The answers were very telling! Not tattle-telling, just "telling." One friend was hesitant to comply. She argued that, because she didn't want any negative feedback from anyone else, she would not want to deal any out. She would rather just talk if I wanted to.

I told her, "Well you are always welcome to give me any verbal feedback anytime and all the time that you wish! But this I am asking you. I'm making a very direct request that, as my friend, you would please take the time to do this in my requested method, format, and timeline."

It was important that she trust me in my thinking that it was both necessary and helpful to me. I reminded her, "If you think it won't be helpful to tell me anything that's negative, think of it like this: At a dinner party, I have a big chunk of spinach in my teeth. Of course, I want you to tell me about it so that I can remove it before I give my big spinach-y grin to everyone there. After all, I want people to remember me for who I am, not the distracting vegetation I unknowingly showed off. I really am asking for brutal honesty. You are my friend, and I need to be able to count on you for it. It's extremely helpful for me to know and consider aspects of myself that I cannot necessarily see with my own eyes."

This interaction alone was beneficial because it let our relationship grow to a place where we reaffirmed we both wanted honest and helpful feedback from one another. Now we don't doubt that door is open for either of us; and as a result, I feel a deeper friendship with her than ever before.

Another friend told me it seemed I was always trying to explain myself. She said that sometimes it was hard to be in a conversation with me for that reason. Ouch! Although this was hard to hear, it helped me come to grips with some people-pleasing tendencies I had. I began to recognize I had paid too much attention to what people think or might think. When I took a long hard look at myself and my part in some conversations, I was continually trying to derail potential negative thoughts someone might develop about me. It was at an extremely ridiculous level, and it was exhausting me.

I was so shamefully grateful to have received this feedback, though, as strange as that may seem. It hurt. I was embarrassed. Importantly, though, I was enlightened to how I sometimes came across. Somehow, I knew this was an ugly part of me that took up too much of my time and energy as well as keeping me stuck where I wasn't tending to the things in life that were really important. Worst of all, I wasn't always fun to be in a conversation with! This was a huge lesson.

People-pleasing is very curable. A simple read through the Book of Proverbs and any number of other scriptures in the Bible will get us on the right track.

The fear of man lays a snare, but whoever trusts in the LORD is safe.
Proverbs 29:25

Many seek the face of a ruler, but it is from the LORD that a man gets justice.
Proverbs 29:26

How can you believe, when you receive glory from one another
and do not seek the glory that comes from the only God?
John 5:44

When a man's ways please the LORD, he makes even his enemies to be at peace with him.
Proverbs 16:7

With helpful feedback about my huge people-pleasing blind spot, I had the opportunity to grow into a person who didn't have to spend so much time worrying about what others thought. I learned to let my "yes" be yes and my "no" be no. Because of this somewhat painful awakening, I slowly overcame the desire to explain myself all the time for any and every reason. Ultimately it was liberating!

But above all, my brothers, do not swear, either by heaven or by earth or by any other oath, but let your "yes" be yes and your "no" be no, so that you may not fall under condemnation.
James 5:12

TELL-TALES, SAILS, AND DRAG

Life has enough drag of its own. I think we owe it to ourselves and others to reduce the amount of drag in our lives by trimming our sails, so that we are actually having the effect we want to have and think we are having. How often do unnecessary, unhelpful misunderstandings have drag on our lives?

LET'S SAIL-IBRATE!

We can live and communicate efficiently without unnecessary breakdowns in relationships and treat each other well and in a way we would want to be treated. We can make a commitment to adjust the sails so we can make good use of the available wind, go where we want to go, and get there before it's too late. Especially in our relationships, let's make them as good as we can early on. As an older gentleman I knew used to say, "My wife and I have been happily married for 10 years. We've been married for 40, and by year 30, we finally figured it out."

Here's a quick thought about who to ask for feedback: ask people whom you love and who also love you. Asking someone to tell you something difficult to hear about yourself is a large request. It's an important job, and this task should not be given to just anyone. People need to love you enough to not be critical for the sake of being critical. Also, they cannot be people who would be afraid of your backlash if you were not mature enough to hear what they have to say.

Whom in your life could you ask for honest feedback about how you relate in relationships? Friendships? Work relationships? Spousal relationships?

If you are struggling with deciding whom to ask, check out Cloud and Townsend's book *Safe People*.

PRAYER

Father, we thank You that we can come to You for feedback, and thank You that You have provided us a way to get feedback in our relationships. Sometimes we feel so very tired, frustrated, and worn out in our efforts. Sometimes we are tempted to feel hopeless, that things in our relationships will never get better. But we know we should find our value in You. Thank You for helping us to find our value in You and You alone! We know from Your Word that You have great plans for us, to prosper us and not to harm us. We know You will also help us prosper in our relationships with ourselves and with others. Thank You for wisdom about whom we should trust when seeking feedback, and thank You for opening our eyes to what You want us to see about ourselves. Thank You, most of all, for showing us the truth that sets us free! We want to Sail-ibrate freedom! We love You and thank You for all these things in the name of Your Son Jesus Christ.

CHAPTER THIRTEEN

GETTING LOST ... THEN FOUND

One of the worst feelings in the world is being adrift and not knowing where you are headed. When a major storm forms right on top of you—like I've experienced a couple times both in the literal and figurative senses—it can really throw you off course and put you into a desperate situation. I'd always considered the start of my career at the aquarium a great God story, and it had afforded me a place from which I could do something I absolutely loved and help people and animals along the way. I worked hard, was loyal, and pursued growth both personally and professionally. Nevertheless it ended abruptly. It could have been one of the worst days of my life. Here's how it all went down.

DEATH OF A DREAM JOB

It was a long, adventurous, happy, painful, amazing, interesting, fun, exhausting, and prestigious thing that came to a screeching halt that day. It was the end of a 12-year era—more than a third of my entire life at that time. Losing my dream job was something for which I was not ready. Not that I didn't see it coming, but I was definitely not ready, nor would I ever have been. It felt as though I had been married to this place, but things had been very rocky lately. I'd fought for the relationship but got rejected anyway. The morale was at an all-time low after a two-year downward spiral. After being called into the office, thanked for my service by a temporary director, and told I had about 20 minutes to get my gear and clear out. I was completely numb.

Events from the last 12 years were flashing before my eyes. Images of animals and conversations with people who were like family to me for over a decade were swirling around in my head like a tornado, and I could hardly think. Originally from the corn fields of Indiana, I had been living my dream as a marine biologist at an aquarium in Florida, doing animal care, research, field work, grunt work, and trying my best to help people along the way as well. Having my position cut was certainly a colossal loss! Fearful that my heart COULD NOT sustain this damage, I somehow kept breathing…and moving. My dream job…wasn't this supposed to last a really, really long time? My role was something I'd so proudly let define me. This job, this place, I'd made my purpose! Now what?

In all of my urges to panic, freak out, or say angry or sad things to people I passed as I exited the building, I somehow stayed in the frozen state of 'just keep moving'—the reptilian part of my brain was kicking in to just survive the next couple minutes. These were important minutes, I knew; but somehow, at the same time nothing seemed important.

I could not even think. How I was supposed to get into my car and drive at this point was beyond me, but somehow in the next 30 seconds I would have to figure it out. Key, door, open, sit, start, seatbelt, reverse, forward… drive. Trying to aim for the unemployment office I struggled to pay extra attention to the things that normally would've been automatic—like safe driving and maintaining awareness of where I was and where I was going. I was numb.

In the next quarter-of-an-hour car ride, I managed, under great duress, to have one of the most profound conversations with God I've ever had. "Okay, God, where's this all going? Other than a really loud audible answer from you right now, which I know I may not get, I'm just going to breathe and listen for any hints from you that things are going to somehow be okay and eventually good or maybe even great again someday."

My next question was to myself. What's my plan? Of all the revengeful ideas swirling around in my head, I knew enough to try to keep those out of the immediate decision-making effort. I willfully decided that, despite the fact the world had just crumbled down around me, I would tell God I was going to continue to trust Him with my future. Trust God.

I really wanted to believe, despite this disaster, that God had some really awesome plans for me; and somehow the future could be even better than the past. I had also known I did not want to stand in God's way of blessing me with good things. I had grown a bit in my walk with God; but coming from some past situations where bitter was better, it would have been all too natural to spit venom at my accusers, reach for revenge, and try to get some heads to roll.

I'd run into that wall before. I knew all too well from failure after failure that it's harder for God to bless me and bring about good things in me and my situation when I'm focused on past hurts and immersed in the pain of trying to somehow get even. When I've been angry and mulling over scenarios of revenge in my mind, it's been hard to keep a lookout for God's provision. Even worse, however, was the temptation to hang on to the idea that I am the victimized one. Which, I was, for right now.

"God, I want to trust You. I want You to take me where You want me. I have no foggy idea where that is, but please, please, please show me You have great big plans for me. Tell me about the next adventure we can have together. Or even for now, just tell me THAT we will have a great adventure together. I know You give so many wonderful promises to those who choose to follow You. Not a life of comfort, but of richness and joy (and maybe some justice and vindication!?)." I was so scared. And I had no idea how He would actually pull that off...any of it! How do you even get there from here? I mean, He is God and all, but from where I sat, things looked REALLY BLEAK.

I took a deep breath, terrified of each approaching minute, and drove on, not expecting an answer anytime soon. To cut the silence, I turned on the radio.

Yep, more outrageous than a famous cliché, the song that played made me burst into tears... of joy. A new one, "More" by Matthew West. Singing as the voice of God to his beloved ones, he sings, "I love you more than the sun and the stars that I taught how to shine, you are mine and you shine for me, too. I love you, yesterday, and today, and tomorrow —I'll say it again and again... I love you more!

WOW!!!

Even though it was something as simple as the right song at the right time, it was clear that was Him speaking to my heart. The Creator of the Universe loves you and me like THAT! And it was enough to help me turn the rudder of my attitude from a dangerously downward direction to one that could catch the uplifting winds of hope and aim me in a better direction, instead of a bitter one. Adjust my attitude, adjust my altitude.

Looking back, I have to say I am so grateful for what God has done for me since then. And I'm very glad not to have missed out on the many awesome things I would have had I chosen bitterness instead of hope. Although days, weeks and months were very hard after that day, it was always forefront in my mind to cling to the Hope God had given me. I didn't want to stay bound to the past and its bitterness. I wanted to be propelled forward by clinging to the Hope of a good future.

God has since guided me to much bluer waters than I could've ever imagined and has restored and advanced me in my career in ways I could not have dreamt. Blessings are not in short supply in heaven or on earth.

What were some of the tough times God saw you through?

What is part of your story that can become a useful piece of gear for someone else's journey?

Let us cling to these things when new challenges and difficulties hit so we can be resilient and not shaken. There is a saying that goes: "Don't doubt in darkness what God showed you in the Light."

"For I know the plans I have for you," declares the LORD,
"plans to prosper you and not to harm you, plans to give you hope and a future."
Jeremiah 29:11

Here are the lyrics of the song by Matthew West.

MORE

Take a look at the mountains

Stretching a mile high

Take a look at the ocean

Far as your eye can see

And think of Me

Take a look at the desert

Do you feel like a grain of sand?

I am with you wherever

Where you go is where I am

And I'm always thinking of you

Take a look around you

I'm spelling it out one by one

[Chorus]

I love you more than the sun

And the stars that I taught how to shine

You are mine, and you shine for me too

I love you yesterday and today

And tomorrow, I'll say it again and again

I love you more

Just a face in the city

Just a tear on a crowded street

But you are one in a million

And you belong to Me

And I want you to know

That I'm not letting go

Even when you come undone

[Chorus]

I love you more than the sun

And the stars that I taught how to shine

You are mine, and you shine for me too

I love you yesterday and today

And tomorrow, I'll say it again and again

I love you more

I love you more

Shine for Me

Shine for Me

Shine on, shine on

Shine for Me

[Chorus]

I love you more than the sun

And the stars that I taught how to shine

You are mine, and you shine for me too

I love you yesterday and today

And tomorrow, I'll say it again and again

I love you more

[Chorus]

Than the sun

and the stars that I taught how to shine

You are mine, and you shine for me too

I love you, yesterday and today

Through the joy and the pain

I'll say it again and again

I love you more

I love you more

And I see you

And I made you

And I love you more than you can imagine

More than you can fathom

I love you more than the sun

And you shine for me

PRAYER

Father, thank You for loving us in all of our ups and downs and in our joys and woes. Thank You that our identity and our purpose is in You and not what we do. Thank You that You make known to us the path of life and in Your presence there is fullness of joy; at Your right hand are pleasures forever more. (Psalm 16:11) Thank You that You love us more than the sun and the stars and the most magnificent things of creation, and we are the objects of Your affection. Thank You that our real purpose, real value, and real worth come from You. We love You. Thank You for righting our wrongs, covering us with your grace, shaking the dust of life off of us and bringing us closer to You. Thank You for making us to shine for You. Thank You for awakening us to the identity and purpose You have given us, in the name of Your Son Jesus Christ.

PART THREE

FULFILLING OUR MISSION

CHAPTER FOURTEEN

BE HEALTHY TO LIVE OUR PURPOSE

To live out our purpose, we have to strive to be healthy in every way we can. We can strive to be spiritually healthy, physically healthy, mentally healthy, emotionally healthy, relationally healthy, financially healthy, vocationally healthy, and verbally healthy. All of these areas can and do have an impact on our effectiveness as humans, especially when it comes to our living our purpose. Sometimes we struggle in one area but have smooth sailing in another. It happens, we are human. I have struggled with each of these during my life, and not just a few times. It has helped me immensely to view each of these areas in terms of healthiness and to identify the respective reasons why health in all of them is our goal.

Spiritually healthy: So that we are transformed, informed, guided, and motivated by our connection to God and His Son; so that we can speak life into this world; and so that we do not live in the ways of the world.

But you are a chosen race, a royal priesthood, a holy nation,
a people for his own possession,
that you may proclaim the excellencies of him who called you
out of darkness into his marvelous light.
1 Peter 2:9 ESV

Physically healthy: So that we can get around and go where God needs us to go, have energy and focus, and be responsible stewards of the body we were given.

Do you not know that your bodies are temples of the Holy Spirit, who is in you, whom you have received from God? You are not your own; you were bought at a price. Therefore, honor God with your bodies.
1 Corinthians 6:19-20

Mentally healthy: So that we know God's truth, can discern truth from lies and choose life for ourselves and others.

I call heaven and earth to witness against you today, that I have set before you life and death, blessing and curse. Therefore, choose life, that you and your offspring may live.
Deuteronomy 30:19

Emotionally healthy: So that we will not be hindered by the temptations to freeze up, hide, live under oppression, be parked in the past, or be bound by bitterness.

Therefore, since we are surrounded by such a great cloud of witnesses,
let us throw off everything that hinders and the sin that so easily entangles.
And let us run with perseverance the race marked out for us.
Hebrews 12:1

Do not be anxious about anything, but in everything by prayer
and supplication with thanksgiving let your requests be made known to God.
And the peace of God which surpasses all understanding,
will guard your hearts and your minds in Christ Jesus.
Philippians 4: 6-7

Relationally healthy: So that we love wisely, forgive thoroughly, have healthy boundaries and supportive, rich, genuine relationships.

Be kind and compassionate to one another, forgiving each other,
just as in Christ God forgave you.
Ephesians 4:32

I, the LORD, search the heart and test the mind,
to give every man according to his ways, according to the fruit of his deeds.
Jeremiah 17:10

Financially healthy: So that we can be good stewards of the resources available to us, allowing us to sustain ourselves, be generous, make our own choices, help loved ones and others in need, further God's kingdom using our gifts, providing resources, and being obedient in spending, saving, and investing.

Be sure to know the condition of your flocks.
Proverbs 27:23

Give, and you will receive. Your gift will return to you in full–pressed down, shaken together to make room for more, running over, and poured into your lap. The amount you give will determine the amount you get back.
Luke 6:38

...be on guard against every form of greediness, for one's life does not consist in the abundance of things he possesses.
Luke 12:15

Vocationally healthy: So that our days are filled with choices and efforts that produce good things for us and others.

Whatever you do, work at it with all your heart, as working for the Lord, not for human masters, since you know that you will receive an inheritance from the Lord as a reward. It is the Lord Christ you are serving.
Colossians 3:23–24

Then some soldiers asked him, 'And what should we do?'
He replied, 'Don't extort money and don't accuse people falsely–
be content with your pay.'
Luke 3:14

Verbally Healthy: So that we are using our words and conversation to align with the power of God's creative language rather than working against it.

From the fruit of their lips people are filled with good things,
and the work of their hands brings them reward.
Proverbs 12:14

Equally as powerful as the work of our hands in bringing goodness into our lives, is the power of our tongues. If God is wanting to bless us and not curse us, we should speak the same over our lives and those we love.

Being healthy in all of these ways not only sets us up for a successful lifestyle but also keeps us more in shape to love God, show God's love to others, and work with Him in obedience. In summary, we are to love God with all we have from every area of our lives.

...You shall love the LORD your God with all your heart,
and with all your soul, and will all your strength,
and with all your mind; and your neighbor as yourself.
Luke 10:27

We are given a simplification blanket that covers everything. Love God with everything we have and love others as ourselves.

We should love God spiritually, physically, mentally, emotionally, relationally, financially, vocationally, and verbally.

We are responsible for so many aspects of life. We are not perfect, but we are powerful. Even when we do not feel powerful, our choices are powerful toward one end or the other. When we realize our power of choice, our purpose, and our potential, we have motivation to maximize what we are and what we have in God's purposes. He will guide us and He will help us. He will also give us rest, security in Him, and a hope for a wonderful future.

Let's ask ourselves these questions.

In seeking excellence in the pursuit of God and my purpose, in what area would I like to grow?

In which realm of life would even a small change afford me more freedom?

What is one small thing in each area mentioned above, I can do right now, that would put me on a healthier path toward loving God, myself, and others well?

This week, what three areas can I make a small change in that will be helpful to me?

PRAYER

Father, we ask You to help us to be healthy in every area. Help us to be spiritually healthy, physically healthy, mentally healthy, emotionally healthy, relationally healthy, financially healthy, vocationally healthy, and verbally healthy. Thank You for prospering us in every area and for bringing us to new and more powerful levels of health so that we can powerfully live out our destinies and fulfill our purposes in You. We ask You and thank You for all of these things in the name of Your Son, Jesus Christ.

CHAPTER FIFTEEN

KEEP A LOOKOUT

FOR GOOD THINGS COMING YOUR WAY

A story of how God works in healing our relationships.

Years ago, out of the blue, I received an actual "Dear John" letter in the mail from my best friend, Morgan. It was so out of left field I couldn't even comprehend the words I read in her lovely handwriting. The anger came up and off the page and seared my heart to a crisp. I was horrified to read about this "monster"… me. I was selfish, greedy, not there for her when her father died. (WHAT? I didn't even know her father had died! I was finding out as I read the letter! Oh my God!). She'd criticized me, my life, my boyfriend at the time, etc. I can't even remember the rest because her last words were "good-bye" and "never contact me again because any further communication would be awkward." Awkward!?

I dove right in to awkward. Our relationship was worth it. I called,

I begged, I pleaded, and I wrote letters on postcards, so that her whole family could see I was trying to make amends. I didn't want the story to get twisted so that I was made to look the bad guy in the eyes of others, too! It's bad enough to lose a friend like this; but additionally I worried about looking bad in the eyes of everyone else. Oh, how messy we humans are! I was also hoping if others knew I wanted back into this relationship, I'd have others on my side who could influence her judgment and help her get to a different verdict. What a royal mess.

I thought long and hard, and was at first very angry at her for developing this story without me. I simply had no say! And her dad died and oh my, why did she not tell me? She had left me a couple phone messages (the general kind—not the "my-dad-is-dying" kind) so I just didn't call back. First, I wasn't good at communicating. I was very self-absorbed with my job; I was a workaholic at an aquarium. I was also in a pretty deep funk. I had a weird thing going on with my voice where I had strained it so badly the doctor ordered me to not talk, utter a peep or even whisper for two long months to avoid further damage to my vocal cords. Honestly, I didn't call anyone back during that time; but I realized I could've had my sister call her to tell her that I couldn't talk. Really, I had lots of help from people who stepped in and were willing to do my bidding during these difficult months. Nevertheless, responding to her was not my priority. I was very busy, you see. It seemed I was getting a lot of pool time but not the fun, vacation-type pool time. I was either drowning in a pool of watery responsibilities at work or a pool of self-pity at home.

Looking back, I really was kind of a jerk. Absolutely, I contributed to this broken relationship in more ways than I had wanted to admit.

However, I had let myself off the hook in numerous ways. I can be really good at excusing my own behavior.

I missed my friend Morgan deeply. We were besties. When my mom died after I'd just turned twelve years old, Morgan and her family were there for me in ways my own family couldn't be. Together, we got through high school and college and God-only-knows the many and frequent shenanigans that permeated that time of life. After college, she traveled to visit me at my new residence. She even fell in love with the aquarium where I worked and loved visiting the marine animals, especially one of the dolphins who was trained to paint by holding a paintbrush in his mouth and smearing brightly-colored paints on a canvas. Morgan grew to love marine life so much that she actually had a marine-themed wedding! I couldn't believe that I'd lost her.

After a handful of unfruitful attempts to reconnect, I slowly, despairingly gave up.

Ten years passed.

I walked out of a very deep prayer time at a Christian conference where I had been particularly praying for healed relationships in my life. My prayers were not focused on Morgan, since I had long given up hope on that relationship. Truthfully, I had several newly broken relationships; it was getting hard to keep up. My prayer time was about a lot of people: family, friends, ex-friends, future friends, the whole kit and caboodle of relationships of which I wanted good ones. I truly wanted to succeed at this relationship stuff, and I needed God's help in transforming this area (and so many other areas) of my life. I had to surrender to the idea I was falling short in multiple ways that badly affected all my relationships. I began to repent of my slacker ways. I had to begin to push pride aside and realize I really was no award winner when it came to this stuff. I had been guilty of selfishness, self-centeredness, and being a good friend only when it was convenient for me. I was a mess, but I wanted to be the type of person through which God could bless others.

After that prayer time, I turned on my phone to find a single voicemail…from Morgan! The cell phone almost slipped out of my hands. I fumbled with fear and excitement as I managed to get the phone to my ear to listen to the message.

She wanted to connect with me again because she started to realize she had unfairly blamed me for everything that was wrong in her life during a very dark time, and she wanted me back in her life. Oh my God, the sweetness of our first conversation in 10 years was a fountain of life for me. As she walked me through the ways her heart began to soften toward me, I was astounded to see how God had His big, beautiful fingerprints all over it!

Morgan had started to think of me as from time to time various reminders of how we were connected would come to her mind. She explained she just started feeling the urge to forgive what she'd held against me for so long. For many years, she thought about me but couldn't bring herself to make the contact. Even her husband started urging her to contact me. She told of little promptings she'd feel to forgive me and how she was encountering little and large reminders of our friendship; she had started to miss our friendship but was still trying to dig in her heels and not cave in.

Then came the event that sealed the deal in her heart that we absolutely had to make amends. Her seven-year-old daughter, whom I'd not yet had the chance to meet, brought home a children's book from the school library (in Indiana) about a wonderful dolphin who lived at an aquarium in Florida who could paint. "Isn't this amazing, Mommy? I would love to see this dolphin some day!" she exclaimed.

Morgan smiled really big and told her daughter, "Yes, honey, I know that very dolphin; and I think I know just the person who could introduce you to him!" As Morgan relayed all of these amazing details to me, I could tell that her heart was smiling nearly as much as mine was.

Then, she asked me a question for which I was unprepared. "Where are you if you are not at your place?"

"What?" I asked.

She answered, "Well, we are all here at your place and knocked on the door; but it doesn't look like you are home. We brought the kids down to visit Florida to meet the artistic dolphin and wanted to surprise you! We head home the day after tomorrow."

I could hardly speak. "I'm at a Christian conference in North Carolina and am heading home the day after tomorrow," I responded.

We laughed at the apparent untimeliness of her being at my place after all these years, and my being away at exactly the same time. We agreed to get together as soon as possible and have the warmest, sweetest reunion ever! And we did. We picked up right where we had left off 10 years earlier.

Now, we are closer than ever, as if no time had passed, and have the strongest bond, unwilling to let it get shaken again…ever…over anything.

When God helps you heal, it's real. Although you may see evidence of an old scar, the hurt has been healed as if the wound hadn't occurred.

Consider all the areas God is ready and waiting to heal in us if we come to Him with our hurts.

With whom in your world do you desire a healed relationship? What are you willing to forgive to have it?

For what are you willing to ask forgiveness?

What is the unspoken conversation that will set you free?

What wonderful things might God have in store for you if you were to surrender some of your hurts, repent of your failings and ask Him to intervene?

God can heal us and our broken relationships. When we allow Him to heal us, we are better able to help others in seeking and accepting His healing as well.

PRAYER

Father, You know all the ways we fall short or miss the mark. You know our every sin, every transgression , and every iniquity that has been a part of us or come before us in our bloodline. You know how ignorance, selfishness and pride have damaged our relationships. We repent of our sins, known and unknown, because we want to be people that are forgiven and free. Thank You for helping us to see what You need us to see to grow into who You want us to be. Father we ask for Your healing and restoration in our lives, especially in our relationships. Help us to be the people You've called us to be; and help us to have whole, healthy and life-giving relationships. Help us be this to others, and help us to find and keep the people who will be this to us. Father, we thank You for restoring and healing our relationships in the name of Your Son Jesus Christ.

CHAPTER SIXTEEN

BE BUOYANT

Have you ever tried to hold a beach ball underwater?

Anywhere you look, in any field, there are life lessons. Being a water girl, aquatic ideas don't ever get old for me.

Take the word "buoyancy." For a mermaid like me, this hosts an important image for my reflections on life, because it's a quick reference of how we interact with principles that operate in the world. Things that are buoyant float; they rise to the top. They are entities different from the environment around them. The concept of *Buoyant Force* was originally described by Greek mathematician, Archimedes, who made his amazing discovery while bathing; and in his "Eureka!" excitement, he jumped out of the tub and ran naked down the street to tell the world about it.

Dictionary.com defines **Buoyancy** as:

The power to float or rise in a fluid; relative lightness. The power of supporting a body so that it floats; upward pressure exerted by the fluid in which a body is immersed. Lightness or resilience of spirit; cheerfulness.

Buoyancy involves an object's weight and the weight of the fluid it displaces. Low pressure objects like a balloon or a buoy filled with air float atop water, which is heavier or denser. In fact, a buoy's natural state is floating atop water. Think of even trying to hold it down underwater. That takes a remarkable amount of skill, coordination, and effort. Then, when you take your hands off, up it goes! Its natural state is up.

Think for a minute…an enclosed area of low pressure, surrounded by an environment of high pressure. When we ourselves are low pressure (aka at peace), we tend to rise above things that are high pressure. This is pretty good incentive to work to maintain our own peace, our low pressure.

Yes, we want to accomplish things; yes, we want to make an impact; and yes, we are all limited by the amount of time we have to do so. However, keep in mind that we ourselves benefit in our personal peace, and therefore our endeavors, when we remain at low pressure. In high pressure environments, as any chemistry buff will know, particles and molecules are moving fast. When in low pressure, they slow down.

As you know, many things in our world tend to increase our pressure; in my opinion fear and unforgiveness top the list. There are also a great number of associated things like anger, jealousy, bitterness, resentment, and grief. The list goes on. You can probably add a few items.

God tells us to be still; a few great examples include:

Be still and know that I am God.

Psalm 46:10

The LORD will fight for you; you need only be still.

Exodus 14:14

Be still before the Lord and wait patiently for him; fret not yourself over the one who prospers in his way, over the evil man who carries out evil devices.

Psalm 37: 7

Being still allows for clarity and discernment. I wish I could remember where I heard the following analogy.

Think of a glass bowl of dirty water. (I always think of a fish bowl full of dirty water that has been shaken or stirred—not with the fish in it, of course.) When left to be still and not agitated, the dirt particles will settle to the bottom. The result is clarity of the water. Profound, right?

Creativity is more accessible to us in low pressure conditions. When we can take time to really see things; be unhurried, playful, or relaxed; and look for ideas, new angles, and fresh perspectives, we are more able to focus. When we focus on what's most important, we can choose where we apply our attention and energy, and we can then create.

We can create…

A life lived on Purpose.

A life of purpose where we live intentionally and not reacting to everything around us.

A life that is full of thoughts and actions that are helpful for moving toward fulfilling God's destiny for our lives.

A life focused on the purposes of God's Kingdom and our role in it.

A life that is effective for being a functioning, contributing and supportive member of the Body of Christ.

We are more effective, helpful, and impactful when we are aware of the reality of the situation before us. We are able to listen more effectively when we are operating out of a low-pressure state than when reacting from a high-pressure one. When we have a sense of purpose we desire to stay low-pressure; and that allows for the natural upward movement, like a buoy. If we match the high pressure that we perceive around us, we will simply blend in and be no higher than what we subject ourselves to or what we see in others. We want to let ourselves rise above the norm. Rise above the status quo. Rise above where we've settled before. Rise above where we've previously let ourselves get stuck. Be buoyant.

How about Psalm 23?

The LORD is my shepherd, I shall not be in want.
He makes me to lie down in green pastures,
he leads me beside quiet waters, he restores my soul.
He guides me in paths of righteousness for his name's sake.
Even though I walk through the valley of the shadow of death,
I will fear no evil, for you are with me;
and your rod and your staff, they comfort me.
You prepare a table before me in the presence of my enemies.
You anoint my head with oil; my cup overflows.

Surely goodness and love will follow me all the days of my life,
and I will dwell in the house of the LORD forever.

Take another look at the verse that says, "you prepare a table before me in the presence of my enemies."

There is an amazing audio teaching by John Schoenheit of Spirit and *Truth Fellowship International* that talks about this idea.

Talk about high pressure! There might just be a major storm going on. Enemies are nearby. Impending danger is all around. Somehow, I'm supposed to have a seat, relax, and enjoy some refreshments! That sounds like I'm supposed to be enjoying a low-pressure moment in the midst of a high-pressure environment! Although at a glance this may sound crazy, no doubt a major challenge if not impossible; God wouldn't tell us this if it were not possible. He made us and he knows our propensity to react to the world around us. He knows what and how we feel. He tells us in a myriad of ways throughout the Bible He has and is what we need no matter what we are going through. In Psalm 23 alone, He tells us in about a dozen ways just how he will take care of us!

- He is my shepherd
- I'll not be in want
- He makes me lie down
- He leads me
- He restores my soul
- He guides me in righteousness (for His name's sake, not mine!)
- I don't have to fear evil for He is with me
- He comforts me

• He prepares a table = He provides for me… even though there are enemies

• He anoints me and keeps my cup overflowing

• He assures me that goodness and love will follow me all my days

AND

• I have a guaranteed spot in His eternal household!

Slow down, take a breath, bask in these ideas. Daydream about what this means. Meditate on these truths. Ask God for wisdom. Ask Him what this means for you. Yes, He means this good stuff for you! Listen, really listen and be open for the peace He is trying to transfer to you.

Let go of your anxiety so you can fill up on His peace. Let's say "no" to the twisting, competing, unruly troubles that are flopping around. Trying to deal with something we are not meant to deal with can be very frustrating. It's like trying to hold a sack of raccoons. Let's put down our sack of raccoons so we can take the pillow He is offering us. Make the trade. It's definitely an up-trade, AND it's already paid for.

What can you and God create together in the moments of high pressure?

Something to consider: When you rearrange a couple letters in the word REACTING, you can make the word CREATING. Nice, huh? Just don't run out of the tub naked to tell the world like Archimedes did.

PRAYER

Father, thank You for making the Universe and all we see and know. Thank You for making me ; You know all about me, my sitting up, lying down, how I was formed in the womb and everything I could possibly encounter in life. Thank You for helping me encounter You and Your presence in a way that keeps me low pressure. Help me to be aware! Please take my tendency for stress and high pressure and trade it for Your peace. Teach me to hand it over to You and not take it back! Lead me into Your peace, help me to recognize Your gently leading above the temptation and noise of anxiety. Thank You Father, in the name of Jesus Christ for helping me to be buoyant and low pressure no matter what's going on around me. Help me to be calm, unshaken and effective for Your Kingdom.

CHAPTER SEVENTEEN

HAVE SOMETHING IMPORTANT TO SAY

Don't do it. Don't fuss. Don't whine. Don't gossip. It's all a big waste of time at the least; and at the most, it causes a ripple of negative crap that can come back and bite you in the butt or cause grief for others. Trust me, I know.

The value of words was and is more than I ever knew.

In my mid-twenties, I lost my voice for two entire months. After a common cold and maybe a little fever, too, I kept over doing it. I kept moving, kept working and kept talking…even with my sore throat and raspy, failing voice. I had to. You know, people and animals depended on me. I didn't want to wimp out. I didn't have time to rest. There were sick dolphins to care for, stranding response teams to keep moving, volunteers to supervise, projects and tasks to coordinate, and basic needs to be met. There was always something seemingly more important than my taking care of me. I did not have time to get sick or the luxury to be voiceless. Or so I thought.

After a run to the doctor, who sent me to an ear/nose/throat specialist, I found nodules had begun to form on my vocal chords; and I should not speak for two months…not even a whisper! Apparently, whispering is even harder on your voice than regular speaking. I was not prepared for this. How would I even function? I suppose it could be worse. The part of me that wants to be in control of things was just not happy! "What on God's green earth am I supposed to do?!" I asked, with my last little attempt of a verbal request.

The Doc said, "NO TALKING," and he quickly and preemptively held up his hand and shushed me as soon as I began to utter the word "really?"

"Shhhhh!" the doc said as he handed me a big pad of paper and a pen. "Really," he said, "for a minimum of two months."

"Fine!" I wrote.

It was brutal. The first week was very, very long and harsh. I had to learn that I just could not even utter a peep. Oh, the pent-up thoughts swirling around my head wanting to be released. I had to just breathe, smile, and cry, silently, of course. I was quite saddened by this new, hopefully only temporary, change; and I would periodically wrestle with denial. It was annoying in every sense.

The next couple of months were interesting. I had to make do. I wrote on a big dry erase board in the aquarium food prep room that I was supposed to be silent and would be communicating for a while in only silent forms. I had to explain this nonverbally to about 80 people over the course of the first week. I wrote in big, resentful words. Every new day, I mourned the fact that I would not be able to personally describe in detail to any of them the whats, whys, and hows of the day. In a very short time, I had to get good at communicating things with as few words as possible. Time would simply not allow for more; and the writer's cramp would be unbearable. Wow, was this a challenge! I had to be concise, polite, and receptive for questions without the normal verbal part of conversation. For smaller, more detailed things, I'd carry my notepad with me.

With some silent frustration, I somehow got better at not having to get in the last word. A little part of me died every time I had to forgo this gratuitous and guilty pleasure. I had to let go of the desire to comment on anything and everything. I had to think very carefully about what I wanted to say, because communicating now came with a cost I was not accustomed to paying. I had serious choices to make—only the most important, helpful, and effective words. I learned, even when I thought I really needed to give input, conversations got along without my having to say it all. That lesson was humbling.

A very wise retiree volunteer had been telling me to slow down and stop trying to do it all. "The cemeteries are full of people the world couldn't live without!" he told me. I was being forced to listen…and observe. From a painfully restricted point of view, I began to slowly see the world a bit differently. I had to give up some control and just be helpful.

The world didn't need my every comment. Less was more. People did need guidance and wisdom. Not always from me. I needed wisdom; and, boy, did I start to get a dose of it.

I had to watch life happen, but I could only participate silently. After a while, it became entertaining. I would write a question to someone at work; and instead of answering verbally—as they could at will—some would grab my notepad and begin to write the answer before laughing at themselves and speaking the remainder of the response. It was funny. Additionally I was forced to learn how to attend staff meetings where I was unable to verbally add information or defend myself or my department. I noticed fewer criticisms and accusations than usual, perhaps because folks knew there would be no defense. It was interesting to see that things got along without continual verbal input from me. Long afterwards, even after my voice returned, I continued to enjoy being relatively silent in staff meetings.

The Bible provides great reminders what our thoughts and focus should be:

Finally, brothers and sisters, whatever is true, whatever is noble,
whatever is right, whatever is pure, whatever is lovely,
whatever is admirable—if anything is excellent or praiseworthy—
think about such things and the God of peace will be with you.
Philippians 4:8

And it also instructs us about the kinds of things we should say...

Do not let any unwholesome talk come out of your mouths,
but only what is helpful for building others up according to their needs,
that it may benefit those who listen.
Ephesians 4:29

What great instructions! We have the ability to keep ourselves in check. Most would probably accept and live by this teaching without the serious 'reminder' I needed.

I quite often reflect on my time of silence, and I am grateful for it. I myself heard the wasted words of others, while shamefully remembering so many of mine. I also saw the effect of well-placed words on others. What an eye-opener and a mouth-shutter!

I would encourage everyone to indulge, for a while, in some prescribed silence—or at least fast from all complaining. How long can you go without uttering a complaint? Try it, even for a single day. If you fail, try another day and then another. Try as many as it takes. Do this, and I imagine you will reap massive benefits. I have.

Start over when you mess up. I still fail and make stupid comments. There is no need to beat ourselves up over it. That's not helpful. Let's learn to recover quickly and remember to correct our attitudes and language. It will help us stay focused on what is needed… and helpful.

Death and life are in the power of the tongue,

and those who love it will eat its fruits.

Proverbs 18:21

PRAYER

Father, I ask You to teach me the power of Your words and the power of mine. Help me have wisdom and to understand the true creative value of words; also teach me how I should use them to speak about my life, the lives of my loved ones and the lives of everyone I encounter. Thank You for giving me wisdom and discernment about what should be spoken and when. Help me to use my words to build up and not tear down. Help me to use my words powerfully, effectively, and beneficially for Your children and Your Kingdom. I ask and I thank You for this in the name of Your Son, Jesus Christ.

CHAPTER EIGHTEEN

WATCH YOUR LANGUAGE

Have you ever been on a sinking boat? I have. It was one stormy day with two very trusted coworkers, a jetskier, a shrimp boat, the USCG, an island sandbar, and the initial reason for being out on the boat that bad weather day—a beached dolphin. Although the title of this chapter may appear to be a lecture about cussing, it is not. (Incidentally, there are not only a few cuss words flying around when you are on a sinking boat.) The chapter title and the real point, however, is that what we say to God, ourselves and others is extremely important. Not only in a crisis situation, but always. This is true every single day. Our words, like God's, are to bless, to echo God's Kingdom, to declare what heaven would have on earth, to cover and intercede for those around us, and to prepare others' hearts to awaken to God's call.

For the Word of God is living and active and sharper than
any two-edged sword,
and piercing as far as the division of soul and spirit,
of both joints and marrow,
and able to judge the thoughts and intentions of the heart.
Hebrews 4:12

We humans share with God the ability to speak in words. God's words have creative power. And God tells us we are partakers in the use of words.

But I say to you that for every idle word men may speak,
they will give an account of it in the day of judgment.
For by your words you will be justified,
and by your words you will be condemned.
Matthew 12:36-37

From the fruit of his lips a man is filled with good things
as surely as the work of his hands rewards him.
Proverbs 12:14

What we say is very important to God; and therefore, it is very important to us and others. Speak as if your words matter; because they do. For better or for worse, they matter. It is good news, however, that all the good things we say will remain to benefit us.

Then those who feared the Lord talked with each other,
and the LORD listened and heard. A scroll of remembrance was written
in his presence concerning those who feared the LORD and honored His name.
Malachi 3:16

JESUS IS OUR REAL CAPTAIN

In the sinking boat scenario, we used our words to ask for help from the One who walks on water and calms the waves. We asked for miraculous help; we also asked Him what to do to avoid getting totally swamped.

To each other, we used our words to encourage. We reminded ourselves God was ready to help us, we had equipment and knew how to use it, and we could take the right opportunities when necessary… and would somehow be okay. Although some things went wrong that day to put us in that desperate situation, many things came together to bring us out of it. At day's end, I was thrilled to be alive and back on land.

A good man brings good things out of the good stored up in his heart,
and an evil man brings evil things out of the evil stored up in his heart.
For the mouth speaks what the heart is full of.
Luke 6:45

We have to have goodness in our hearts in order to be verbally healthy. That comes by putting God's Word in our hearts and enjoying a relationship with our Creator and Savior. To develop a renewed mind and transformed heart requires time and persistence; until then, we can make an effort to line our language up with God's.

Your words are currency;
Be careful how you spend them.
VALORIE BURTON

Will we spend our words to bolster God's case for us or the enemy's case against us? Will our proclamations resemble God's or the devil's? Our words have the creative power to make or break us. Our words can be used as a pathway for God's promises or display disbelief or lack of faith in His goodness and intent. God says He desires to bless us; yet, if we continually say things like,

"Nothing ever goes right for me" or

"Love never works out for me,"

how do we expect God to feel? "How I wish these kids would understand how much I love them and go along with My plan to bless them!"

I know many people who proclaim that, by having low or negative expectations, it's more of a pleasant surprise when something positive happens. Of course, they also say believing that is easier than being disappointed when good things don't come. That attitude is potentially a cowardly avoidance of what God actually says and a careless disregard for God's directive disguised as logic. God says,

"For I know the plans I have for you," declares the LORD,
"plans to prosper you and not to harm you,
plans to give you hope and a future."
Jeremiah 29:11

God knows more about our psychology than we do, and He's given us key promises and guidance so we can rise above the suggestions of the world.

Although hard times come, as the Psalmist says:

Surely your goodness and love will follow me all the days of my life,
and I will dwell in the house of the LORD forever
Psalm 23:6

or

You make known to me the path of life;
you will fill me with joy in your presence,
with eternal pleasures at your right hand.
Psalm 16:11

Let's take God at His Word that we have a powerful and creative impact to make on the world. Let's line up our language to look like His. Let's speak life, encouragement, strength, comfort, healing, and love into our lives, those of our loved ones, and in our communities. Let's honor the authority of Jesus Christ by proclaiming his authority over us, our circumstances, and our situations.

There are many great, inspiring resources on using our words to bless others. For one, *The Gift of the Blessing* by Gary Smalley and John Trent, Ph.D.

PRAYER

Father, thank You for giving us the ability to speak life as You do. Thank You for giving us as believers in the Body of Christ the ability by our declarations to make a real and lasting difference in people, and therefore the world. Help us to be always mindful of our potential impact on others as we see great visions for them; let us make great declarations over them. Teach us to be strong mentors for those we can bless. Let us show Your light and reveal Your truth to those who need it. Thank You for the privilege of using our words and the authority of the name of Jesus Christ to pave the way for blessings for others and ourselves. Thank You for all these things in the name of Your Son, Jesus Christ.

CHAPTER NINETEEN

LETTUCE REJOICE

IN TAKING OPPORTUNITIES

I was recently talking with one of my transformational coaching clients; and she was expressing how, especially lately, she felt she was missing opportunities. This feeling is one I battle as well. How often does an opportunity pass right by and, only after it passes do we see it for what it was? This is the back end of opportunity, and I am so very familiar with it.

How often have I failed to listen carefully enough, observe non-judgmentally enough, or step even a little outside of my business-as-usual comfort zone? How many times could I have easily encouraged someone who desperately needed it? How often have I failed to meet a need that would have cost me little? In how many situations might I have served someone powerfully by taking a moment and mustering even a bit more courage? What smidgeon of extra kindness could have made a real difference to those who needed to know they were on the right track?

In the rear-view mirror, I have seen more of these opportunities than I care to admit. In fact, it's rather difficult to consider, just how many times I have simply "missed it." I know I have to forgive myself and move on, continuing to look for new opportunities… unless I want to miss more of them. If I'm stuck in my own failings, I simply cannot pay attention to the present moment; I would be taking myself out of the current game if I keep replaying the last one.

When we sometimes miss opportunities, though, God will help us see them more clearly when we ask Him and make an effort to follow His lead.

Right here, in the present moment, is our next best decision. It's within our reach. Here is a good example from when, somehow, I managed to 'nail it.' I was actually paying enough attention to make a difference for someone, and I ended up with more than I bargained for.

I was supervising about 80 volunteers, at the small aquarium in Florida, in the general care and feeding of the animals. In the mornings, the food prep room was abuzz with 6-10 people weighing and chopping the fish that would be fed to many creatures, including dolphins, sea turtles, otters, fish, sharks, stingrays. In this not-for-profit environment, where we relied on hundreds of volunteers doing myriad jobs, I was responsible for multiple departments, safety requirements, personnel issues, and more. It was all too easy to fall victim to the "I'm-way-too-busy-for-this-stuff Syndrome." My sleep-deprived-slap-happy condition from staying up all night with a sick dolphin added to the chaos.

One of the simple tasks we'd give the new interns was to make bi-weekly acquisitions of lettuce from the local grocery store for our resident sea turtles. It was an easy job. They would call the grocery store, ask for our non-cash donations of the green stuff, pick it up, label it, store it in the right place, and then divvy some of it up to the hungry swimming beasts. Although it was an easy task, I always personally walked them through it the first time. We had a good relationship with the store and wanted to show the interns how to interact with outside businesses as a representative of the aquarium. In other words, we wanted anyone making the calls to be courteous, respectful and grateful. This new intern was a gem, and I knew she would be easy to train. She was trailing close behind me entering the food prep room as I explained the process of her new responsibility. I showed her where to look on the wall above the phone for the number to the Publix produce department, and began to dial. Everybody in the room—the volunteers, dolphin trainers, biologists, and animal care team members—naturally quieted their banter while I made the call.

An unfamiliar female voice answered, "Hello?" That's weird. Could I have misdialed? I've probably dialed the number thousands of times—a t least two or three times a week for the better part of a decade—and it was highly unlikely I dialed the wrong number; however, while odd, I suppose it could happen.

Slightly off guard, I gingerly asked, "Is this the Publix produce department?" The voice said, "No, this is Sophie…I'm at Morton Plant Hospital."

Very surprised, I said, "Oh, I'm sorry; I was trying to reach the Publix produce department." This is where I heard a little voice inside me say, "Slow down … take a minute… listen…"

Slowly I proceeded, "Sophie at Morton Plant Hospital, huh?" "Are you a doctor or a patient?" I really had no idea what was coming next but thought I'd peek down the rabbit hole and see. "I'm a patient…room 362, bed 2," Sophie replied.

By now, every eye in the room was looking at me, each face with a different expression, mostly with curiosity. "What are you in for, 'Sophie in room 362, bed 2?'" I asked. She answered, "I have this rare disease called Guillain-Barre' syndrome. I am paralyzed and the doctors don't know for sure if I will ever walk again. I've been here for two weeks, and I'm very scared."

This was getting weirder by the minute. "Guillain-Barre syndrome?" I said slowly, recalling every detail of the only Guillain-Barre syndrome story I was told by a friend of the family, whose son had this strange affliction as a child years prior. He is walking around just fine these days, but it was quite a scare, I remembered.

"Sophie, I know someone who had that very same illness; and he is walking and even running around just fine these days, as he has been for the last 40 years. It took him six weeks to recover, but he did! And you will also!"

By now, every mouth of every person in the food prep room, especially that of my new intern, was hanging open in shock at this exchange.

Sophie's voice was cracking, and I could hear her choke back a few tears as she said, "Oh, thank you; I am so relieved to hear that! I've been so scared," she gulped, "and worried. I was getting so depressed! I'm so glad you called today! You are a God-send, and this is just what I needed to hear! Who are you?"

I told her who I was, where I worked, and whom I was trying to call before I "misdialed" and got her.

As this phone exchange ended, those in the room began firing questions at me.

"What in the world was that all about?!"

"Who is she, how did you get her on the phone instead of the grocery store, and WHAT in the WORLD is *Goolin Berry Syndrome*?!"

"How on God's green earth did you know what THAT was or that she would WALK again?! "

"If it were anyone else in this room…? – well none of us has ever heard of *Goolin Berry Syndrome*. It sounds like Sophie was lucky it was you who dialed the wrong number; but apparently it was the RIGHT number!"

For quite a while in our food prep room, laughter, cheering, and reveling in the shared great experience of Sophie walking again abounded. I was so glad, despite my countless previous missed opportunities, this time I had seen and taken the chance to hit a home run by slowing down, following God's lead, listening for what opportunities were present, and, therefore, bringing some encouragement to a person who desperately needed it. (You really can't make this stuff up!) Smiling to myself about being able to bless someone, I started walking out of the room, when my slightly distraught intern said, "Well, what about the Publix lettuce? Aren't you going to show me what to do?" Oh yeah …

Making life as simple as we can enables us to live at the pace of love and make a powerful impact at every opportunity. Slow down and look around. What opportunities are right in front of you?

Remember a time, or the many times, in your life where you ABSOLUTELY NAILED IT! I'm sure there have been some great ones.

That is who you are! You are able. You are ready. You are uniquely equipped to respond, to provide, to encourage, to add joy or hope to someone who desperately needs it, and to pour love into a heart that longs for it. At every turn, we have opportunities.

What can you do to show God's love to someone?

What are some of the countless, everyday ways you can make God smile?

Where in your life would you like to slow down so that you can move at the pace of love?

Think of when you 'came through' for God or others that reminds you of who you really are, of your true identity as one of God's agents showing love to others.

PRAYER

Father, thank You for helping me see others as you see them and opportunities as you do. Help me move at Your pace, the pace of love. Help me place my attention where You want it and on what You see as important. Help me notice others' needs and show me where I can help. Open doors for me to help others in healthy ways and lead me with proper boundaries into territories where You've called me. Thank You for forgiving me for the missed opportunities when I've been too distracted, self-absorbed, selfish, prideful, or fearful to consider others' needs as my own. Teach my heart to follow Your lead and help me to be present in the moment so that I can be an encourager, protector, defender, and comforter for people the way You would want me to be. Help me be an integral part of the body of Christ and step into the role You want me to play in Your Kingdom. Thank You for all of these things in the name of your Son, Jesus Christ.

CHAPTER TWENTY

BRING ON THE GOOD NEWS

We were enjoying an absolutely beautiful, peaceful day in the middle of the Gulf of Mexico. But it didn't last long. It was not that the weather changed, but the social climate certainly took a turn for the worse. Instead of getting better, it got bitter.

Some of my colleagues, whom I love dearly, have very different beliefs from mine. On this particular day, their topic of conversation was something very near and dear to my heart; but their view of that topic was the polar opposite of mine. I'm a Jesus freak, and to say they are not is a huge understatement. They were discussing the "ridiculous" ideas that some people have—that God exists and is actually good, and humankind needs a savior.

I am one of those ridiculous people. I believe not only that God exists, but also He is good (really good); and we are in need of, in the most desperate of magnitudes, a savior.

In my mind, it's pretty clear.

1. God is good.
2. The Devil is bad.

We are in an imperfect world and a spiritual war zone where the Devil tries to win us over by convincing us God either does not exist or is not really good. (Remember, that is the original lie he used to tempt Adam and Eve ... in addition to his more obvious, straightforward mission of to steal, kill, and destroy.)

Our lives, choices and actions, other s' choices and actions, the position of our hearts, prayer, obedience to God, and maybe a little bit of happenstance or a few more factors we don't quite understand, all have some play in the details of how life goes.

My coworkers' belief s on this subject highly conflicted with mine, and I found myself in an internal battle of what to do in this heated situation. I mean, sure, my blood was beginning to boil while listening to the ideas and thoughts they were throwing around. Mostly though, I was internally wrestling with whether and/or how to respond. Dare I speak up and calmly try to discuss any of these ideas? I didn't want to back down from defending God. Frankly, the conversation was so hostile and vehement I thought surely I would end up overboard if I spoke up now about any of my beliefs that contradicted their apparently water-tight perception of life. I decided to bite my tongue for a bit, pray, and try to calm myself enough to sense God's lead in what to do or say. It was treacherous territory... indeed, a volatile situation. If what I said was not convincing, I could easily blow it. Who am I kidding? What I could have said would have been not only unconvincing but downright unwelcome! They were together on this…hell-bent on reveling in the ridiculous idea of God!

I prayed, "Dear God, my blood is boiling! What shall I do or say? How long can I or shall I endure this? Is there an open window for me to interject a defense of You?"

Things were intense. Am I a coward? I very much wanted to defend God's goodness, but I also didn't want to try to run the pass forward, get tackled, and miss my opportunity for a good throw later. These were my beloved coworkers, and I hoped to be potentially working with them in this job for years to come. Do I take the risk now or do I just wait for another opportunity? Dear Lord, what's wise here? What do You and Your wisdom say? I don't want to be a coward, but I also don't want to be a fool.

My prayer went like this: *God, please keep my focus on what's important to You. Please don't let me be derailed emotionally and miss Your will in this intense moment. I am desperately asking what to do and intensely trying to listen to what You are saying to me. God please, please help me remain focused on what's important here. What is most important to You? I want it to be most important to me. Please….*

The conversation kept rolling downhill at breakneck speed, although I was less panicky as I waited for my answer. I continued to scan with my set of binoculars as we continued our search for whales, dolphins, or other marine species I was hoping to get an awesome revelation of what to do; and it would amaze them with God's love at best, or, at the very least, I would survive this day. Things were tense, and I knew I needed some relief.

Where was the pressure valve?

God, again, I don't know what else to do other than ask you to please help me not to unravel. Please keep me focused on what's most important. I kept my mouth shut and waited.

Somehow, I was able to disconnect from the conversation. I was hoping things would die down or we would see something interesting—a welcomed distraction while on watch—so that this painful time-passing conversation would end. There was nothing, but I kept hoping. All I saw on my side of the ship was a smallish long-line fishing vessel. It was on the horizon at the beginning of my watch, and we had gradually moved closer to it. It was a bit odd seeing this small vessel, since we were far offshore in the Gulf of Mexico; come to think of it, we hadn't seen any other vessels in the last couple of days. The boat had been facing mostly toward us but had turned slightly away as we had gotten closer. It was then I could finally discern the name written on the stern of the vessel.

There it was, right on the back written in big, bold, blue letters was "THE GOOD NEWS," the name of the boat and the unmistakable answer to my prayer.

At seeing this, laughter erupted and then tears of joy that I held as tight as I could. My reaction was almost uncontrollable. There in those big blue letters was what was supposed to remain my focus!

Really, God? I was so impressed with His slam-dunk! What an awesome, even impressively sneaky, way to answer my prayer! How did He even pull this one off? Did He whisper in the ear of that boat captain to head a little more to the south of where they normally fished? Did He urge them to leave the dock earlier or later than what they had scheduled? Was the boat just an image, like a vision, shown only to me? No, my coworkers saw it too. Was the name of the boat really something else, but when we looked at it, it appeared to say *The Good News*? Did God prompt me to pray about focus, knowing the answer He had just teed up for me? God only knows.

What impressed me most was how obviously God had been listening to me the whole time and had worked out a way to answer my desperate prayer to remain focused on what was most important. Of course, The Good News was the most important thing. How amazing it was that He was able to bring that message to me in the most surprising and stunningly perfect way for my situation. He put the message right where I was already looking while doing the job I was already doing. How often is that true in life? It all came together for me then. I was not necessarily supposed to say anything during the God-roast. There would be another, more intimate setting to individually exchange ideas with my colleagues; and later there was such an opportunity with each of them intimately and individually. In the meantime, while waiting for His instruction, God helped me to be patient and then thoroughly amazed, even amused. I frequently draw on this story to remind myself God is at no creative disadvantage when answering my prayers or yours.

Do you have a story about one of your tough situations where God really came through for you?

What if we waited confidently instead of anxiously for God to answer our prayers?

PRAYER

Father, we turn to You in our struggles and storms. We cry out to You when we feel persecuted for our beliefs and positions. We know You know how that feels better than we do. Let us be people of love in all circumstances. Let us be resilient when we are, or feel, attacked; and let us be filled with Your wisdom and discernment about how and when to respond. Let our experiences and identity in You, God, become our credibility. As in Matthew 5:16, *let our lights so shine before men that they may see our good works, and glorify You, our Father in heaven.*

CHAPTER TWENTY-ONE

PROVIDE REFRESHMENTS

A long time ago I invited God to seat someone who needs something from me in the airplane seat(s) next to me. "Needs" is a broad term. I didn't mean someone who needs money or riches, but something I can provide through my presence or conversation. I had in mind things like comfort, encouragement, prayer, wisdom, company, inspiration, my own peacefulness or silence, or whatever might serve as a blessing to him/her during the flight. I wanted to learn to listen to God and see how I could love people, even when we were only strangers sitting next to each other for a relatively short period of time.

I love people, and I love giving encouragement. On some flights, I may not have a seatmate, or there may not be anything special going on, so I just read or nap. Napping or reading is the backup plan to the primary objective of interacting in a kind way. By being willing to put others first if there seems to be a need to do so, I have to say I've been amazed more than once by my interactions.

I've sat next to many kinds of people, as anyone who travels regularly has. One of my funnier flights took place shortly after I rejoined the dating scene. I was seated between a female professional matchmaker and a drop-dead gorgeous guy who was studying to become a Catholic Priest. I know, it sounds like the beginning of a joke. (I cannot make this stuff up.) We three had some memorable conversations. Occasionally there are non-interactive people working on their computers or reading, etc., which is an open invitation to zone out... which is, any day of the week, okay by me.

Most of the time I am seated next to people going through real-life struggles: kids traveling alone, those suffering from a tragedy, those grieving a loss, someone hurting from a fresh breakup, or someone terrified of flying. On two different flights within the same month, I sat next to a man on one occasion, and a woman the next, each on his/her way to drug or alcohol rehab. They are both to this day on my sister's prayer list; I can hardly wait to hear how their lives have been affected by God's action as a result of her prayers. I was simply the middleman there; however, I am thankful to have been part of God's process. We do some sowing, we do some watering, and we do some reaping, but not always together.

I was flying home recently from a job. I had settled into my seat—the second or third to last empty seat on the plane—all the way at the back, row 29, seat E, in the middle... the least-favorite seat on the whole plane. (The very last row is, in my opinion, the worst row, because it's just in front of the lavatory, where you can smell the not-so-lovely aroma whenever the door opens. And did I mention it was in the middle? Undoubtedly, it was the worst seat on the plane!)

The last open seat, the aisle seat next to mine, was about to be occupied by a woman to whom I thought I could be a blessing. Why? Well, the tears welling in her eyes as she approached were an indication something wasn't quite right in her world. As she sat down next to me, I gave her a warm smile and a little nod hello. I held her gaze a little longer in a friendly way to imply I was open to conversation. She immediately said, "I'm so sorry. You'll have to forgive me. I'm so sad. My mother recently passed away." Yep, she was the one for this flight.

Normally the intended recipient of my assistance is not quite so obvious right off the bat. However, this was a no brainer. I lost my mother when I was only 12 years old, so I have a very special place in my heart for those who are grieving the loss of their moms. In fact, I usually gravitate toward grieving people, perhaps because I've experienced grief first hand several times; and I know how important it is to give comfort. I find many people are quite uncomfortable around grieving people because they don't know what to say or are overcome by the person's sorrow. Many run away, but I typically run toward them.

As we were just getting into conversation, the last standing passenger, a woman, was looking for her seat near us. She told the flight attendant who approached to help her that she thought she was supposed to be in row 29, my row. There was one open middle seat in front of us (row 28), but perhaps people had gotten mixed up. The flight attendant asked to check the boarding passes of us in the last couple rows to figure out who was supposed to be where. She confirmed the passenger on the other side of me was in the seat matching her boarding pass. She then checked mine and indicated, "You are in the exact right seat." Looking at my new distressed friend she said, "Ma'am, you might be in the wrong row." My new friend, while gesturing toward me, said, "Please, my mother just died, I'm under a lot of stress, and I just feel like I need to sit next to her!" The flight attendant reassuringly allowed it and asked the other woman to take the open middle seat in row 28. Everyone was satisfied.

My new friend and I talked almost non-stop during the flight. We talked about moms and prayer and God and healing and family and spousal relationships. Even several situations she was experiencing with her husband were almost congruent to some I was having with my boyfriend. We related on so many levels. It was as if Someone had scheduled our meeting. Overall, it seemed the conversation for both of us was a blessing; but most noticeably, when we disembarked, she seemed much more peaceful and happy than when she first got on the plane.

About halfway into the flight, my friend got up to use the lavatory. As I sat thinking for a minute, it suddenly occurred to me that it was quite odd the way the flight attendant was so direct in stating to me, "You are in the exact right seat." I pulled out my boarding pass to look at it. I hadn't noticed it earlier when I held it up the flight attendant to see. It read SEAT 28 E. What?! I was sitting in 29 E. 29 E was the EXACT RIGHT SEAT.

Was that a divine intervention? Yep. No doubt. The flight attendant was apparently walking to the beat of a good drum. At one time I was suspicious of it, but now I notice it happens fairly often. I simply smile at all the ways God uses in bringing us what we need when we need it and all the creative ways He gets us together with those who need what we have when we are open to it.

A generous person will prosper;
whoever refreshes others will be refreshed.
Proverbs 11:25

When you are willing to refresh others, God says you will be refreshed. It's a win-win situation.

Who around you might be blessed and refreshed by your sharing yourself; your listening ear; your time; your encouragement; and your beautiful, fearfully-and wonderfully-made self?

PRAYER

Father, thank You for all the wonderful people You put in our lives. Thank You for helping us connect to those You know we can help by showing love, compassion, understanding and inspiration. Thank You for blessing us while we aim to bless others. Thank You for leading us and for preparing our hearts to notice others' needs and to follow through with blessing them. Thank You for helping us to be fearless. Thank You for the divine appointments and for bringing refreshment to us and others. We pray, always, in the name of Your Son Jesus Christ.

CHAPTER TWENTY-TWO

FALL IN LOVE

One of the most incredible experiences of my life was George.

It was an intense, all-consuming experience that left me reeling when it ended. He was incredible. He was awe-inspiring. It was hard to take my eyes or hands off of him. He was all I thought about every day, every hour.

He was also the talk of the town. He was in the newspapers, on TV and on the Internet. He was in the hearts and on the minds of everyone near and far who had heard about him. The general public and scientists came from all over to see him, and I had the pleasure of introducing them to him—I met him anew each and every time I did so.

When people asked me if there was a special man in my life, I would smile from ear to ear and with twinkling eyes reply, "Yes, there is! He weighs 1,200 pounds, is bald, and has no teeth!"

He was an infant sperm whale.

What kind of relationship was this? Well, I guess I was kind of a mom to him. He was only a month old. Basically, when all was said and done, I knew him for more than half his life.

Although I have not had any human children of my own, and I typically do not regard animals as children, I would have to say this experience was very close to motherhood. In between the very few hours of sleep I got most nights on a small cot beside the stranding pool or a rare night where I'd pass out for a bit at home in my own bed, Baby George had my full attention. If I wasn't thinking specifically about him, I was thinking about his formula ingredients, how we'd get them, how we'd pay for them, if they'd arrive soon enough, and who was helping to blend his special concoction which we tried to match to momma whale's milk. Were they being careful about the temperature of the thawing squid, the cleanliness of the tube and feeding equipment and the proper care of the blender? (We'd fried four blenders in the first two weeks alone from making 12 liters of baby whale formula every day.) I was also stressed about his next string of visitors and how to keep things calm and quiet for him. If there were to be a press or media visit, would their lights disturb his resting time? I would need to check on that new little scrape on his tail. You see, it is important to walk the whale or dolphin around the pool if he's not swimming on his own; walking him into the circular current of the pool encourages him to begin swimming again. Also, in a round or curved pool, we would vary the direction of swimming so he wouldn't always be turning the same. We tried to keep the water deep enough to have room for the little whale's whole body and to let him move his tail if he wanted to without scraping it on the bottom, but also shallow enough so that the volunteers lightly supporting him would be able to do so with at least their heads above water. Therefore, we had to make sure to schedule taller volunteers on the shifts with shorter volunteers so that, when George was to be walked in deeper water, we could avoid his tail being dragged. Ugh! There was no small number of details to consider... one day at a time, one shift at a time, and one hour at a time.

George stranded, or washed ashore, on St. George Island in the Florida panhandle. Rescue teams from north Florida responded to a call from people who found him on the beach with an old, infected bite wound on his tail flukes. Perhaps it was a shark or killer whale attack (yes, those can be found in the Gulf of Mexico) that caused him to become separated from his mom and subsequently, wash up on the beach alone. After being examined by veterinarians and loaded into one large rental truck, he was on his next leg of his journey. In the darkest part of the night, two trucks – one from the north (with baby George in it) and ours from the south—lined up tailgate to tailgate and transferred George in the parking lot of an old 7-Eleven gas station, one of two such establishments in the very small Florida town on an unlit two-lane highway. That was the beginning of my motherhood.

How would we deal with him? How could we possibly keep this one alive? He's a baby and should be getting some nourishment from his mother. God only knows how long he'd been injured, scared, and alone. And now he was being poked, prodded, and moved around in another element beyond his control and normal orientation—probably not unlike an alien abduction. The most stable position for him was to lay him on his side. Poor baby. At least he wasn't thrashing around like many other stranded animals we try to rescue. At 800 pounds, he could easily smash all of us. When we got him moved into our truck, we briefed the whole team on who would be positioned where and how to quickly get out of the way if he started to flail around. Safety first.

In most cases it is safest to be kneeling next to the mid-section of the whale or dolphin, usually right by the dorsal fin. You do not want to get hit by a thrashing tail nor bit or hit by the teeth of an open-mouthed, swinging head! Anytime we support and/or move one of these really large creatures, we—by necessity of doing the job—find ourselves in a precarious position. You have to be ready to move quickly, especially during a long transport, if the situation changes.

I recall an instance where we loaded a dwarf sperm whale (a much smaller species of whale than George, the baby sperm whale) that had entered death's throes soon after returning to the facility following a one-hour transport. We had removed into the parking lot all the people from the van to give him some space, calm and quiet while waiting for the vet to gather all the blood tubes and needles ready for a blood draw. After all had exited the step van through the front side door or tailgate, I stepped down from the tailgate with one foot, turned, and stood close by to keep an eye on the dwarf sperm whale while everyone got organized.

I will never forget what happened next. Without so much as a wind-up, the whale lashed his tail (basically the whole lower half of his body) sideways and upward with such force and speed, I saw the new one-foot-diameter dent on the inside of the metal van wall at the very same time I jumped because of the loud slam it made! Of all the dangerously memorable close calls with an animal, I remember that one as if it were yesterday. I tried not to think about that for too long. Fear doesn't help, especially in an already tenuous situation. You stand a pretty good chance of getting by safely if you do the best you can, calculate your risk responsibly, keep everyone safe, avoid doing anything stupid, and be vigilant of where you are at any given time.

George was a different animal. In the few instances in human care, sperm whales, although very large, had not been known to be especially reactive or panicky; consequently we felt a little less threatened. George was very gentle, but his 800-pound body could still squash a person. The priority for the next few hours with this beast was safe transport back to our facility. He lay on his left side atop of a few large foam pads. The van floor was metal; and with the combination of a little blood running from his tail wound, some liquid feces (from the whale, not us), and lots of water from wet towels and sprayers we were using to keep his skin wet, our transport became extremely slippery. The team member driving the van had been informed that slamming on the brakes was not an option. If any of the traffic lights we passed through turned yellow upon approach, we were to keep going and lay on the horn; needless to say, this heavy, wet, slippery mess could become extremely dangerous if we began to slide.

We made it back to the aquarium safely and enlisted the manager from the boatyard (one awesome dude!) at 3am to operate the boat crane so the whale could be lifted over the walls of the rescue pool. He also helped us daily in weighing the big baby to make sure he was gaining, or at least holding, his weight. The help we had in this endeavor was tremendous. What people wouldn't do for this baby whale!

The normal protocol is to euthanize large whale calves, because over the long term, they don't do well without a mom and are not able to be released without a mom or a social group. It was requested that a team of scientists were to be flown in from Hawaii to conduct some specialized, but non-invasive, data collection on this baby's hearing and ability to produce sound. Then September 11, 2001, stormed into existence, shocking the world with tragedy and infamy and delaying any possibility for travel. That week rolled by seemingly slowly, with our becoming ever more attached to our little charge and negating any chance of euthanizing him.

We cared for George for 43 days during which time, he gained 400 pounds. George eventually died due to complications from the lingering infection from his tail wound. During those 43 days, however, I had what seemed like a million moments of "pinch me—I can hardly believe I'm walking, feeding, holding, playing with, weighing, drawing blood from, preparing food for, being pooped on by, and comforting during a thunderstorm a baby sperm whale." Most people don't have the opportunity to see one of these creatures during their lifetime, let alone experience the personal, intensive care process with one.

People have often advised me to write a book. In fact, the father of one of my interns mentioned this while watching us walk baby George around the pool. I was instructing his marine-biology, college-student daughter on what to do as my assistant when her father called down to me from the top of the tank, "You really need to write a book. I hope you know that. If you don't already know it, I'm telling you!"

I replied, "Well, I have to say that I'm rapidly becoming convinced of that. Thanks for saying so."

Very importantly and repeatedly, I came to the realization that, all of us— yes, all of us—have truly amazing stories to tell. Sometimes they involve unusual animals or rare events; but sometimes they include the simple yet miraculous happenings of everyday life, or the blessings of the social bonds and connections we share with others that are so crucial to our wellbeing.

We all have real stories to tell. There is someone, probably many someones, who would be blessed by some of your stories. Let's tell them.

What about your life or experience would benefit others?

When I review or tell this story—or so many other stories—I'm inspired with thankfulness for all of the experiences I've had. It also helps me see through a lens of humility, as I did nothing to cause this event; I was simply a willing participant who was wowed by God's creation and enjoyed a unique place in an interesting, challenging and rewarding story.

Which of your stories are reminders to you how incredible life can be?

What are some of your truly special stories that others would be blessed to hear?

What perspectives or life experiences helped shape who you are?

What have you been part of that you can share to bless others?

PRAYER

Father, life can be an adventure. Thank You for rich experiences that draw us ever closer to You. Thank You for protecting us and preserving us in so many various situations and predicaments. Thank You for grace and mercy amongst dangers known and unknown. Thank You for experiences that have helped to shape who we are today that can be useful to You and Your Kingdom. Thank You for helping us to humbly share with others what would be helpful and inspiring to them. Let our experiences and identity in You become our credibility. Let us be witnesses of Your generous provision and kind character to others. Thank You for all these things in the name of Your Son, Jesus Christ.

CHAPTER TWENTY-THREE

MAKE WAVES

We have been given an opportunity to join God on the greatest Voyage ever taken—our lives. We were made by a brilliant, powerful, creative, loving God, who knows us and loves us beyond what we can even imagine. He created the universe and all that we see… and then some; and we have been invited to be part of His plan. By the very virtue of being alive and able to make choices, we have creative power. We have an extremely important role to play in the greatest story ever written. Let's leave a wake of blessings and deliverance everywhere we go.

Let's dive in to our purpose. When we do, I think we will find we can have a ripple effect that will last into eternity.

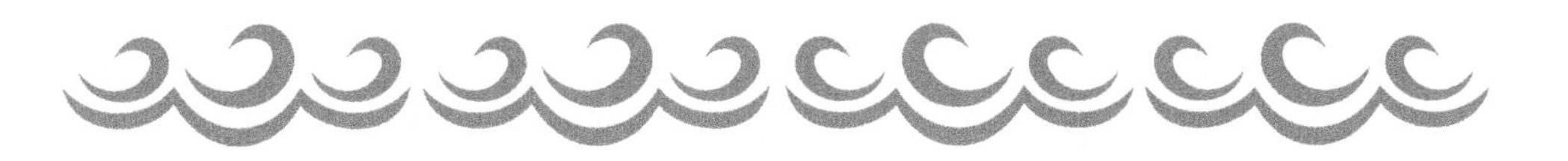

MELODY BARAN

MEET THE AUTHOR

Melody Baran is a marine biologist who specializes in marine mammal and sea turtle biology and conservation. For over 28 years, she has conducted conservation-based research projects including marine mammal and sea turtle surveys during over 1,500 days at sea. She has more than a decade's experience with hands-on marine animal care, marine mammal and sea turtle stranding response, and wildlife photography.

From the tiniest and most endangered porpoise, the vaquita, to the largest creature on Earth, the blue whale, Melody has researched dozens of marine species and experienced some truly amazing events. The unique and powerful perspectives gained from her adventures with nature always draw her attention back to the Creator of it all.

Melody enjoys coaching others to make the impact they want for their lives and encouraging people to live their God-given purpose. She loves being outdoors (usually on, in, around, or under the water) and spending time with family and friends.

Made in United States
Orlando, FL
16 March 2022